The World of
Watteau

TIME-LIFE LIBRARY OF ART

The World of Watteau

1684 - 1721

by Pierre Schneider
and
the Editors of TIME-LIFE BOOKS

Time Incorporated, New York

About the Author:

Pierre Schneider was born in Antwerp in 1925, came to the United States in 1940 and moved back to Europe in the 1950s; he now lives with his wife and two daughters in Paris. He was graduated from the University of California at Berkeley and received his M.A. and Ph.D. at Harvard University, where he became a member of the distinguished Society of Fellows. Mr. Schneider has been the art critic for the weekly newspaper *L'Express* in Paris since 1958. During that time he also served as the Paris editor for the magazine *Art News*, for which he is now a contributing editor. Mr. Schneider has written for *Horizon* and *The New York Times Magazine*. His books include a study of the 17th Century classicist Nicolas Poussin and a collection of essays on poets and painters.

The Consulting Editor:

H. W. Janson is Professor of Fine Arts at New York University, where he is also Chairman of the Department of Fine Arts at Washington Square College. Among his publications are a definitive *History of Art* and *The Sculpture of Donatello*.

The Consultant for This Book:

Dr. Donald Posner, Associate Professor of Fine Arts at the Institute of Fine Arts, New York University, provided valuable assistance during the preparation of this book. Dr. Posner's special field of research and teaching is French and Italian art of the 16th, 17th and 18th Centuries. He has written numerous scholarly articles and is co-author of a book on the art and architecture of the Baroque period.

On the Slipcase:

A detail from Watteau's painting *Mezzetin* shows the popular *commedia dell'arte* character strumming a guitar. The entire work appears on page 105.

End Papers:

Front: Chalk drawings of actors. The Art Institute of Chicago, gift of Tiffany and Margaret Blake.
Back: A sheet of chalk studies. Ecole Nationale des Beaux-Arts, Paris.

TIME-LIFE BOOKS

EDITOR
Maitland A. Edey
TEXT DIRECTOR   ART DIRECTOR
Jerry Korn   Sheldon Cotler
CHIEF OF RESEARCH
Beatrice T. Dobie
Assistant Text Directors:
Harold C. Field, Ogden Tanner
Assistant Art Director: Arnold C. Holeywell
Assistant Chief of Research: Martha Turner

PUBLISHER
Rhett Austell
General Manager: Joseph C. Hazen Jr.
Circulation Director: Joan D. Manley
Marketing Director: Carter Smith
Business Manager: John D. McSweeney
Publishing Board: Nicholas Benton,
Louis Bronzo, James Wendell Forbes

TIME-LIFE LIBRARY OF ART

Editorial Staff for *The World of Watteau*:
Editor: Robert Morton
Associate Editor: Diana Hirsh
Picture Editor: Susan Rayfield
Designer: Paul Jensen
Assistant Designer: Leonard Wolfe
Staff Writer: John Stanton
Chief Researcher: Martha Turner
Researchers: Yvonne Chan, Adrian Condon,
Susan Marcus, Betsy Rein

EDITORIAL PRODUCTION
Color Director: Robert L. Young
Assistant: James J. Cox
Copy Staff: Marian Gordon Goldman,
Muriel Kotselas, Dolores A. Littles
Picture Bureau: Margaret K. Goldsmith,
Merry Mass, Patricia Maye
Traffic: Douglas B. Graham
Art Assistant: Nanci Earle

The picture essays for this book were written by John Stanton. The following individuals and departments of Time Inc. helped to produce the book: the Chief of the Life Picture Library, Doris O'Neil; the Chief of the Time Inc. Bureau of Editorial Reference, Peter Draz; the Chief of the TIME-LIFE News Service, Richard M. Clurman; and Correspondents Maria Vincenza Aloisi, Joan Dupont [Paris], Barbara Moir, Margot Hapgood [London], Elisabeth Kraemer [Bonn], Traudl Lessing [Vienna].

Contents

I

An Age
of Extravagance

On September 1st, 1715, the Duc de Bouillon stepped out on the balcony overlooking Versailles' Marble Courtyard and uttered the solemn, ritual proclamation: "King Louis XIV is dead!" If one of Egypt's pyramids had collapsed, the world could not have been more thunderstruck. Despite the fact that the 76-year-old ruler had been declining for months, not even his enemies could believe that the end had come at last. "When I heard of the death of Louis XIV," wrote Eugene of Savoy, "I admit it had the same effect upon me as if I had heard of a splendid old oak uprooted and laid flat upon the ground by a storm. He had stood upright for so long!" As he lay dying, Louis had noticed that two of his valets were weeping. "Why do you weep?" he had asked. "Did you think me immortal?" The answer is: yes, they did. And now it seemed that, through some dreadful prodigy, eternity itself had come to an end.

But that prodigy was followed by a still more astonishing one: overnight, although he had been on the throne for more than 70 years, the Grand Monarch, and all that he loved and stood for, were forgotten. Along the route followed by his funeral, refreshment tents were set up; people drank, sang, laughed.

Surprising as this lightning change may seem, it can be viewed as the natural consequence of an implacable logic, the logic of absolute monarchy. Louis XIV *(page 17)*, who made much use of the traditional concept of the Divine Right of Kings—partly because he was convinced of its truth but partly also because he rightly saw it as the tool he needed to lift France out of its state of feudal chaos—came to regard the epithet *"Roi Soleil,"* the Sun King, bestowed upon him by a flatterer of genius, not as a term of praise but as a plain statement of fact.

Like the Palace of Versailles *(pages 18-27)* commanding the stately carousel of its alleys and avenues, the King was the shining sun around which all France revolved. Any man who refused to swell the enormous throng of the court at Versailles, or who left it, automatically incurred the King's displeasure. At the Palace, a man's future was made or unmade according to whether the King nodded at him on his way to chapel or to council. France's nobles were turned into courtiers; that is to say, servants (M. de Bouillon and the Marquis de Gesvres, two of the country's more illustrious names once almost came to blows over the privilege of handing the dishes to the King at supper). The Abbé de Polignac, dressed in his finest, was walking one day with the King in the gardens of Marly when the rain began to fall. Louis affably invited him to seek shelter. "It is nothing, Majesty," replied Polignac; "Marly rain does not wet."

The Duc de Saint-Simon, who bitingly chronicled Louis' reign in his memoirs, wrote, "The abominable poison of flattery deified him in the very midst of Christendom." One bowed to him, one bowed even to the food that he was to eat as it was carried along the corridors. One trembled before "his fearful majesty" as before the presence of God. Indeed, it is sometimes not easy to tell whether the King considered himself as God's lieutenant on earth or God as his own lieutenant in heaven. After hearing the account of the disastrous battle of Ramillies, for example, Louis exclaimed: "What! Has God forgotten all I have done for Him?" Little wonder that all men and all things had, as Saint-Simon put it, "the air of being nothing except through him."

Louis XIV "loved glory; he willed order and rule," the memorialist noted. Order and rule were the tools that made the glory. As a strict geometric pattern subordinated the farthest grove and basin of Versailles' park to the preeminence of the Palace itself, so the rigid social hierarchy converged on the radiant person of the sovereign. Etiquette was the law of gravitation that ordained the court's motions around the Sun King. Nobody, not even he, was allowed to deviate from its immutable regulations. "With an almanac and a watch," said Saint-Simon, "one could tell exactly what he was doing although one were three hundred miles away."

Just as etiquette was the King's instrument for social control and centralization—and it is to Louis XIV's lasting credit as a statesman that he realized that this was what France most needed to become a powerful nation—so regulations were introduced to stamp the mark of royal authority on every industrial, commercial and artistic activity in the realm. And Louis XIV entrusted the task of devising and enforcing these regulations to his most loyal and energetic adviser, Jean-Baptiste Colbert.

Nobody was better prepared to carry it out. When Cardinal Mazarin, who had acted as prime minister during the troubled years of the King's minority, was about to die, he told Louis XIV: "I owe you everything, but I think I am repaying my debt by leaving you Colbert." He was right: Colbert proved to be Louis XIV's most efficient aide in the colossal undertaking of imposing the authority of the Crown on the country. Colbert came from a family of cloth merchants; although Mazarin had exaggerated his own debt to Louis, Colbert did owe all he was to the King, and he knew it. So did the King: he deliberately leaned on the bourgeoisie in his struggle against a French nobility which clung

The Sun King emblem of Louis XIV blazed everywhere on the walls of Royal Residences throughout France. The one above is from the railing of a balcony overlooking the Place Vendôme in Paris, a magnificent square designed by one of Louis' chief architects, Jules Hardouin Mansart. The grillwork on gates and window gratings at Versailles, much of which was also built by Mansart, sparkles with Louis' gilded symbol.

to traditional privileges. And he drew from its ranks devoted, hard-working civil servants such as Colbert who enabled him to execute his grand political design.

Colbert set out to establish royal control over all aspects of life. For every industrial, artisan and commercial activity in the land he laid down a set of rigid regulations: the size, quality, color, shape and price of goods were prescribed. These complex regulations were, one might say, the etiquette of economic life.

Colbert was no less careful in domesticating culture. Louis XIV and he saw clearly the role that art could play as a weapon of propaganda. The visual arts could proclaim the Sun King's majesty, power and splendor in the face of the world. Painting, sculpture and tapestry came to be dominated in form and in content by Louis XIV. The works of the period were, in the truest sense of the term, command performances. Almost every statue, picture, table or platter glorified the King. When his victories were not shown directly, they were represented indirectly through legend or mythology; the *Roi Soleil* was celebrated under the guise of Alexander or Apollo, often with naiads, nymphs and fauns chained to the royal walls and to royal furniture as vanquished foes were often pictured shackled to a triumphant conqueror's chariot. An art devoted first and foremost to the glorification of an absolute monarch needs artists who are skillful, docile flatterers rather than free creators —courtiers of the chisel and brush.

To ensure that the esthetic rules were obeyed, a kind of enforcement agency was also needed—a royal bureau of standards, so to speak, for the arts and letters. Now, just such an institution existed, at least embryonically: the French Academy. It had originated about 1635, when a group of French writers had been accustomed to gather in the house of a colleague. The meetings became regular but remained private until Cardinal Richelieu, Prime Minister to Louis XIII, granted the group the title of Royal Academy and gave it official protection. Protection, of course, eventually meant control—and through the Royal Academy, strictly dependent on royal orders, the government kept a watchful eye on France's literary production. By 1648, the Royal Academy of Painting and Sculpture was founded and it came to serve the same purpose as its literary predecessor.

Both institutions suffered an eclipse during the chaotic years between Louis XIII's death and the assumption of personal power by Louis XIV. But now Colbert revived them and endowed them with all the powers needed to lay down the rules and see that they were dutifully followed. The Academy drilled these rules into the heads and hands of a generation of young artists who knew that attending its courses was the surest way to be, someday, elected to membership. And once a man was a member, the Academy continued to remind him of these imperative principles through its regular sessions—attendance at which was compulsory—and its formal lectures. To disobey the principles proclaimed by the Academy was to risk incurring its displeasure, which, in turn, meant losing royal commissions. And that was most unpleasant, for Colbert, who controlled the major commissions of the time, made artists largely dependent for their livelihood on the King's pleasure.

The rules professed by the Academy composed a doctrine, now generally called French classicism. It stated that the laws of beauty were eternal and that the ancient Greeks and Romans had come closest to capturing it and were therefore to be imitated scrupulously—as were those moderns who came closest to the ancients: Raphael, the three Carracci and, above all, Nicolas Poussin. Classicism favored historical painting and the most "noble" subjects. It decreed the superiority of idea over appearance and of line over color. Finally it affirmed that the aim of art was not primarily to please but to instruct.

The man whom the Academy worshiped as the very incarnation of its doctrine was Nicolas Poussin, not only the greatest French painter of the 17th Century but a determined individualist whose love of freedom led him to live and labor in isolation. True, he was a "classical" painter, but for him classicism was not a set of pat recipes but the uncertain reward of a never-ending struggle. He was born in either 1593 or 1594 in a small village on the edge of Normandy, near Les Andelys, of a bourgeois family fallen to peasant status. The long, hard road which he had to travel is strikingly summarized by the inscription which he placed in his self-portrait: "Nicolaus Poussinus Andelyensis Academicus Romanus" (Nicolas Poussin of Andelys; Academician, Roman). He set himself incredibly high aims. Dissatisfied with the watered-down, distorted, provincial version of Renaissance painting prevailing in France around 1600, he chose to go back to the source, and the source was Rome.

He was about 30 when at last he reached it, in 1624. Painstakingly, he hammered out the fine metal of his ideal: to others the gods and heroes of ancient Greece and Rome were mere mythological trappings; to him they were reality. So great was the moral tension and spiritual gravity of his paintings that his conviction proved contagious: thanks to him, the public fancied that the creatures of Olympus and the men of ancient times *(pages 28-29)* lived again.

From Norman peasant to Roman master hailed by learned connoisseurs as "erudite," Poussin had come a long way indeed. His secret? A combination of high purpose, relentless dedication and modesty. Asked what had been the key to his success, he replied: "I have neglected nothing." Yet the humble flavor of Les Andelys is never quite effaced by the grandeur of Rome. Orpheus plays his lyre with the same homely gesture with which the farmer in *Summer,* a nostalgic evocation of Poussin's youth, plays his bagpipe. If Poussin's Latin strikes us as being so alive, it is because he spoke it with the accent of his native Normandy.

And this independent, unbending genius was to be the model for the training of servile, flexible talents! How little he himself was fitted for this role we know, for in 1640 he was called to Paris from Rome, where he had been living for more than 15 years, by Louis XIII. He was appointed the King's First Painter and showered with honors and riches. Yet two years later, he left again for Rome. "I have never understood what the King wanted of me," he wrote some time after. The answer was simple: the King wanted him to become his artistic eulogist, to

Nicolas Poussin, whose classical style became the standard for French art during the reign of Louis XIV, gazes out of a self-portrait that his contemporaries praised as a fine likeness. The stack of canvases behind Poussin identifies his trade.

elaborate a truly royal decor. Poussin, however, could not reduce himself to the ancillary role of a decorator. He renounced the vast walls of the Louvre which he had been asked to embellish and restricted himself to easel pictures, small but filled only with his personal world. He died in the Eternal City in 1665—just about the time the rising Sun King took the reins of government into his own hands.

Louis XIII had vainly expected Poussin to play the part of royal decorator: Louis XIV and Colbert found the right man in Charles Le Brun. Interestingly, Le Brun was an ardent admirer and disciple of Poussin, whom he had accompanied back to Italy in 1642. In every essential way, however, he differed from his master. Nothing had come easy to Poussin, but Le Brun's facility was breathtaking. At the age of nine, he modeled clay and sculpted. At the age of 12, he was already a skilled painter, protected by influential patrons. Moreover, Le Brun had none of Poussin's intransigence and independence of spirit: he welcomed Louis XIV's offers with eagerness.

He had all the scope and stimulation he could wish for. Colbert appointed Le Brun what we would call today Minister of Cultural Affairs —a minister with dictatorial powers over the artistic production of the realm. Not only was Le Brun named First Painter to the King and Director of the Royal Academy of Painting and Sculpture, he was also in charge of the Gobelins, the factory where the famous tapestries were woven and the royal furnishings were made. Here were employed France's finest cabinetmakers, goldsmiths, artists and artisans of every sort. Le Brun commissioned, controlled, coordinated, corrected. Better still, with staggering energy and facility, he painted the frescoes of Versailles' Salon of War, Salon of Peace and Hall of Mirrors *(pages 24-25)* —comprising one of the supreme artistic achievements of the *Roi Soleil*'s reign—and he provided designs for tapestries and for spoons, for garden and fountain statuary, for the embellishment of the King's ships, for his tables, chairs, chandeliers, for the frames of his mirrors and the façades of his palaces, for his door locks and even for the carriage which he sent to India as a present to the Great Moghul. Directly or indirectly, he was responsible for the creation and triumph of that stately, decorous, heliocentric idiom known as *le style Louis XIV*.

Its characteristics were, in the words of Saint-Simon, "splendor, magnificence, profusion." Pointing to the King's mantle in the portrait by Le Brun, the Duc de Grammont exclaimed: "There is a mantle that may rightly be called a hyperbole in velvet." The art of Versailles was a hyperbole in marble, gold, brocade. Every table was as pompous and solemn as a march by Lully. Every bed looked like an altar, every armchair like a throne. The majesty and luxury were crushing: at Versailles, the solid silver chandeliers were so heavy that not even the strongest man could budge them. The flower beds at Versailles and Trianon were changed every day (to make this possible thousands of flowerpots were kept in the King's hothouses). On some days, the scent of tuberoses was so overpowering at Trianon that the King and the court were forced to leave the gardens.

Discomfort was, in fact, the corollary of majesty. Mme. de Maintenon, the King's last mistress (and eventually his secret wife) complains bitterly about the glacial drafts that sweep through the King's impeccably aligned state rooms: "For him, nothing counts but grandeur, magnificence and symmetry. . . . One must perish in symmetry." What gives *le style Louis XIV* its power and dignity is that it is self-centered but not self-indulgent, ostentatious but not epicurean. "A prince," wrote Louis XIV in his *Advice to the Dauphin,* "must see in these distractions something else than mere pleasures. Mankind delights in spectacles. . . . Through them, we sometimes control their hearts more effectively than through rewards and gifts; and as regards foreigners, such expenditures, which may seem superfluous, cause in them a very advantageous impression of magnificence, of power, of wealth and of splendor."

Impressive the art of Versailles unquestionably was—and still is. It is a triumph of the will over human resistance (what we perceive and remember are the features of an overall style, not the names of the individuals who contributed to it) and over natural obstacles; the Palace and park of Versailles were wrested, at colossal expense of money and human lives, from sterile, unsalubrious marshland. Like the majestic but empty-eyed statues posted at the crossroads of its gardens, the art of Versailles is at once filled with strength and devoid of humanity. Indeed, the fascination which it exerts may well stem from this deep contrast.

Suns that rise must go down. The year 1686, which saw the completion of Le Brun's Salon of Peace and Salon of War, marked the climax of Louis XIV's reign. But already decline was close at hand. The King's military victories and dreams of hegemony gradually antagonized all of Europe. His bitterest enemy, William of Orange, Stadtholder of Holland, whom he had contemptuously underestimated and who in 1689 was crowned King of England, patiently knit the countries of the continent into a formidable alliance. France was plunged into a series of disastrous wars. Commanded by generals who knew better how to maneuver at court than in the field, her armies suffered badly. The exodus of Protestants, denied by Louis the right to follow their religion, deprived the country of its most industrious citizens. Mismanagement was the consequence of entrusting the reins of the state to men equipped only for flattery. By the turn of the century, France was in steep decline.

With age, the King's defects of character increased and hardened. He resented the slightest criticism, accepted no advice but flattery, and under the influence of the puritanical Mme. de Maintenon, fell into the most intolerant form of bigotry. Henceforth he wore only dark clothes, and he banished from the realm the theatrical troupe of *commedia dell'arte* players whom he had personally protected and loved, because he could no longer brook the salaciousness of their repartee.

Soon France showed signs of "universal bankruptcy." The women of Les Halles, Paris' central market, marched on Versailles to demand bread. On the battlefield defeat followed upon defeat. "Every day brings something new—never good," remarked the Princess Palatine, Louis XIV's sister-in-law. Even nature seemed to have entered into the Great Alliance. A succession of incredibly bitter winters ravaged France. In 1691, to pay his famished troops, Louis sent all his gold and silverware

This detail from a Gobelins tapestry depicts Charles Le Brun escorting King Louis through the Gobelins factory. In addition to decorative wall hangings, the 250 painters, engravers, sculptors, weavers, dyers, cabinetmakers, goldsmiths and embroiderers employed at the Gobelins made nearly all ornamental and practical furnishings for the Royal household. Le Brun designed everything from carpets to candleholders.

—the dishes, tables, seats, chandeliers fashioned by Le Brun and his collaborators—to the mint to be melted. Le Brun himself, half disgraced, half forgotten, spent his final years (he died in 1690) in the Gobelins tapestry works. "At the court, all that remains is sadness, boredom and distrust," wrote the Princess Palatine. And Saint-Simon, even more chillingly, wrote: "All was silence and suffering."

The final blows came in 1711 and 1712. In rapid succession Louis XIV lost his son and successor, the Grand Dauphin, then the Duchesse de Bourgogne, wife to the King's grandson and now heir, and finally the Duc de Bourgogne himself. The cause of their sudden deaths was probably in each case scarlet fever, against which the physicians used the disastrous but universal remedy of the day: bleeding.

The Duchesse de Bourgogne had been the last ray of sun in the King's life. "With her death," wrote Saint-Simon, "joy, pleasures and even amusements vanished, as well as every sort of grace; darkness covered the whole surface of the court." Age—for lions an insult worse than death—held Louis XIV in its claws, despite his courtiers' attempts to belittle the depredations of time. One day at dinner he complained of the discomfort of having no teeth left: "But, Majesty, who has teeth?" the Cardinal d'Estrées replied. The worst was when, at the King's bidding, the court *had* to be gay. The masked ball at Marly which Louis XIV attended dressed in a robe of gauze—he seemed a ghost—and where many of the dancers were paralyzed by age, must have looked like a re-enactment of the medieval dance of death.

Art, naturally, reflected this change. The Gobelins were officially closed down: there were no more royal commissions. Military painters went out of business: there were no more royal victories. The Academy, which had been selecting the themes for its art competitions from the King's glorious deeds, now was forced to switch to the Old Testament (to which it clung till the end of the 18th Century). The bigotry of the latter years of the reign imposed a moral censorship. The Marquis de Villacerf, Superintendent of Fine Arts and Architecture, wrote to the Director of the French Academy in Rome: "You would oblige me if you were to prevent Saint-Yves from copying paintings by Titian in which there are too many naked figures, for the King presently does not much appreciate such things." So little did Louis appreciate them that he even ordered the nakedness of the Gobelins tapestries woven in more tolerant days to be covered with patches.

Artistic activity did not disappear: it shrank and shifted its ground. The two great architectural and pictorial enterprises of those years were religious: the Chapel of Versailles *(pages 26-27)* and the Chapel of Les Invalides. Death itself proved a source of inspiration. There is something funereal beneath the glittering visage of all tyrannies. Solemn, petrified, awesome, the art of Louis XIV was ready for death. The great show was not yet over; it was simply assuming the color and air of mourning. And mourning became the age of Louis XIV: funerals— *pompes funèbres*—were designed and staged by Le Brun and later by Jean Berain, who as painter of the King's "Small Pleasures," was in effect his private decorator. Small pleasures and great demises! The asso-

A food warmer and platter are offered for inspection at the Gobelins factory. Although kitchens and dining rooms at Versailles were so far apart that hot meals often arrived cold, the King was a formidable gourmand. His supper might include four bowls of soup, a pheasant, a partridge, salad, hashed mutton spiced with garlic, two slices of ham, plus pastry, fruits, sweets, hard-boiled eggs and a variety of good French wines.

ciation was quite normal during this period. The words of Bishop Bossuet, Louis XIV's guide in religious matters, in his funeral oration for the Prince de Condé, apply to all the artistic manifestations of those interminable, ebbing years of an overlong reign: "Cast your eyes all about: here is all that magnificence and piety were able to do to honor a hero; titles, inscriptions, vain masks of what is no more; figures that seem to weep round a tomb, and fragile images of a grief which time undoes with all the rest; columns that seem to want to raise to the very heavens the magnificent testimonial of our nothingness."

Louis XIV had been the lid: with his death the kettle boiled over. "Never had one seen so little sadness at the death of a king," wrote a contemporary chronicler. Public dances were inaugurated and held thrice a week at the Opéra, at the Comédie Française, open to anybody for a small admission fee. Debauchery, drunkenness and irreligiousness, hidden under the late monarch, now spread scandalously in the open. As Michelet put it: "The inside has become the outside."

Those years of saturnalia are known as the Regency. Louis XV, Louis XIV's great-grandson, was an infant at his accession to the throne, and Louis XIV's nephew, the Duc d'Orléans, became Regent. This in itself was a kind of divine retribution, for Louis XIV, in an effort to strengthen his own line, had done everything he could to reduce his collaterals and their progeny to utter idleness and insignificance. The Regent did not dominate his age as his uncle, the late Sun King had. "He has much of King David in him," wrote his mother, the sound-witted, homely, German-born Princess Palatine, with remarkable insight. "He has courage and wit; is musically gifted, short, brave, and likes to sleep with all women." The Duke was a glutton and had such a reputation for drinking that an early 18th Century picture representing Bacchus, the god of wine, was long thought to be a portrait of him. Rare were the late suppers at his residence, the Palais-Royal, that did not end in an orgy. He is rumored to have had incestuous relations with his daughter, the even more scandalous Duchesse de Berri, and he unquestionably went in for ostentatious blasphemy. To an old woman, delighted by his unusual concentration at a Christmas service, he explained that he was reading not his prayer book but Rabelais.

It should not be thought, however, that the Regent was a mere bundle of vices. He was exceptionally intelligent, open-minded and cultivated. His interests ranged from chemistry to art. His libertinism itself had positive aspects: in the word "libertine" there is the word "liberty," and it is not surprising to learn that the Regent admired the freedom of England's political and social life. Whereas Louis XIV's majesty awed all those who approached him, the Regent's relaxed ways put everyone at ease. On January 2, 1716, he personally inaugurated the first public ball at the Opéra—and also, in the process, a new age. He was looking down on the dance floor from his loge when someone shouted: "Come on down and dance, Regent!" He did, and French civilization followed him.

The change was evident in every aspect of French life. Physical weight and its moral equivalent, gravity, were replaced by lightness. The armor that the Regent is wearing in his portrait by Santerre seems as light and soft as a suit of satin. The stiff brocades, the marblelike gowns and prisonlike corsets of the age of Louis XIV now were superseded by rippling, fleshlike silk, by muslin and that typical Regency fashion, the *négligé*. The solemn saraband was vanquished by the sprightlier minuet. In furniture too, the hard, the symmetrical, the monumental, the somber, gave way to the undulating, the diminutive, the gaily colored. No more pompous marble pilasters and sculptures, but nimble wood paneling and supple stucco and terra-cotta figurines.

Nothing illustrates the new spirit of the times more strikingly than the meteoric rise and fall of the Regent's treasurer, John Law. The Scottish economist with the somewhat shady past was hailed as a savior by the Regent. The public treasury was empty, commerce had come to a standstill and industry had fallen into lethargy. The remedy proposed by Law was simple: paper money. Its invention and use would have been downright inconceivable in the period of Colbert, who maintained that "silver makes a State's greatness and power." Now it was greeted with wild enthusiasm; and for a while it seemed to work. Inflation revived the nearly inert production-consumption cycle. But it was Law's mistake to link the credit of France's money to the fortune of the flimsy Company of the Indies. The latter promised huge profits in faraway America. Its shares soared and soared. So eager were people to buy them that they hounded Law day and night; one lady even had herself lowered into his bedroom via the chimney to beg him to sell shares to her. Speculation got out of hand, the promised profits did not materialize. When the tide of confidence turned, it did so practically overnight: the Company of the Indies, and with it the French treasury, went into bankruptcy. Law was forced to flee the country incognito, and went to London, leaving behind a distrust for paper money that France has not overcome to this day.

If the Regent sympathized so readily with the intelligent but reckless Scotsman and with his ideas about the flow of money, it was because the latter corresponded perfectly with the age's reaction against the frozen, hierarchic immobility of Louis XIV's reign, and thirsted for circulation in all matters: women, ideas, words—and currency. Nor did art remain untouched by the new spirit. The Regent himself dabbled in painting—significantly, he illustrated the bucolic love story of Daphnis and Chloë—and patronized the arts. Antoine Coypel, his favorite painter, produced for him a work which may be regarded as the very symbol— one might almost say the manifesto—of the revolution in taste under way: *The Loves Triumphing over the Gods.*

For the heroic mode now yields to the amorous, the virile to the feminine. Mythology still is the prime reservoir of pictorial themes, but Apollo and Jupiter retreat before Venus and Diana; vaporous pinks and celestial blues replace the heavy browns and blacks of Le Brun's school. Le Moine's *Apotheosis of Hercules* on the ceiling at Versailles is really the apotheosis of the new taste. "All the figures were in movement," wrote a contemporary, "the sky was of the softest blue, the atmosphere deceptively airy." Lightness, mobility; one thinks irresistibly of Saint-Simon's remark about the Regent: "He could live only in movement."

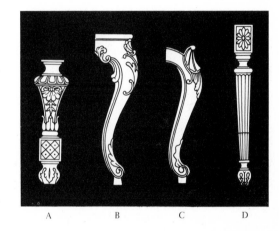

A   B   C   D

Chair legs can proclaim an era's spirit. At the beginning of the 18th Century the chair legs under Louis XIV (A) were straight and heavily ornamented. Under Louis XVI (D) the legs became straight again and severely classical. In the sensuous interval between these two eras (B and C) the legs grew more cabriole, or curvy, and the ornamentation less geometric, more sinuous and floral.

Monument to the Sun King

During most of Antoine Watteau's brief lifetime, the dominating force in both politics and art was the all-powerful Louis XIV *(right)*, who united France, forged a stable government centered on his court, and inspired a decorative style that still bears his name. The light and sensual gaiety of Watteau's paintings found no place on palace walls, for Louis, the arrogant Sun King, wanted art that glorified his power and prestige.

As a symbol of his authority, and to house his many courtiers, Louis created a colossal chateau on the scrubby marshlands of Versailles, some 10 miles west of Paris. To set that vast estate aglow, the King commissioned quantities of brilliance; he delegated the responsibility for designing the setting to architects Louis Le Vau and Jules Hardouin Mansart; to Charles Le Brun, a talented painter with a great flair for management, fell the job of decorating the interiors. The master gardener André Le Nôtre supervised the laying out and planting of miles of parks, paths and formal gardens, as well as the *Orangerie* that Mansart built to house the more than 600 living orange trees which were the King's delight. For over 40 years thousands of workers—craftsmen, artisans and builders—labored to construct a showplace that is a perfect expression of Louis' reign; it is colossal, masculine, sumptuous and imposing. On its completion Versailles became the most gleaming jewel in a diadem of royal palaces that stretched across Europe.

This portrait of the King, full of Baroque swirls, hints at the gay Rococo style that followed his reign. Above the waist, he is all pomp; below, he displays a graceful leg and fashionable slippers—as if he were ready to dance with the new era.

Hyacinthe Rigaud: *Portrait of Louis XIV,*

Sheer size is the first impression conveyed by the Palace at Versailles, as is indicated by the great sweep of the forecourt, the Place d'Armes, in the panoramic picture below. Atop the main gate is a gilded crown bearing the royal fleur-de-lis. Beyond, at center, is the façade of the hunting lodge, built by the King's father, Louis XIII, which forms the core of the Palace. When the King commissioned Louis Le Vau—one of the architects for his residence in Paris, the Louvre—to design new structures at Versailles, the builder preserved that façade and its marble courtyard and simply enveloped the old lodge with his new constructions. Facing toward the rising sun, the buildings flanking the courtyard fall back rhythmically toward the King's rooms.

Some time after Le Vau's death, the architectural work was taken over by Mansart, who designed the tall chapel rising at the right, and added to the garden façade. The huge structure, which covered some 15 acres and housed about 10,000 people, cost six of every 10 francs gathered by the King's tax collectors.

Lighted as it must have been every night of Louis' occupancy, the classically symmetrical west façade of Versailles glitters in one of the two reflecting pools. On their rims sit bronze sculptures representing the great rivers of France. On the second floor of the building, behind regular sets of Ionic columns, is the 239-foot-long Hall of Mirrors *(right)*, which connects the north and south wings. Together with its flanking rooms, the Salon of Peace and Salon of War, the gallery—which has been called the most beautiful room in Europe—occupies the central section of the garden façade and is laid out to reflect the rays of each day's setting sun. The more than 300 mirrors lining the interior wall are set in 17 arched recesses that echo the window pattern. Set in chased copper frames and made in Venice, each mirror cost more than the average French workingman earned in a year.

In King Louis' day the room was sparsely but sumptuously furnished; two large carpets in light colors complementing those of the ceiling paintings lay over parquet floors; silver tables and tubs for the King's orange trees stood about, and 41 silver chandeliers and candelabra lit the room. White damask curtains embroidered in gold softened the window light. But the room's chief color came from Le Brun's magnificent ceiling paintings —a series of large compositions, oval medallions and cameos, telling in allegories the history of Louis XIV's accession to power, his military victories, and his beneficent civil reforms.

As much care was taken with the exterior of Versailles as with its interiors. The Sun King appointed André Le Nôtre to design a new setting and he planned wonderfully varied surroundings: elaborate formal gardens (*above*) flank the apartments; pools, a canal and basins lend relief to the broad alleys leading into parklands farther away from the buildings, and quiet glades stand off the main pathways—all of which obediently lead back to the Palace itself, which is at the center of the entire plan.

Precision, formality and order characterize Le Nôtre's gardens; trees, hedges and shrubs are clipped into geometrical shapes; flower beds are planted in precise patterns; and gravel pathways cut neat swaths into

Martin Frémery: Copy of the Medici Venus, 17th Century

forested areas. They were gardens designed to impress; the Duc de Saint-Simon complained that Le Nôtre's stony paths hurt his feet and that the gardens were places to admire and avoid. But the setting, with its classical statuary and clean-cut lines provides a perfect counterpoint to the buildings of the Palace and makes Versailles a reflection of the great King's glory.

One of the most spectacular of the many dazzling fountains at Versailles is the one in the Basin of Apollo *(above)*, which lies at the end of a long avenue leading up to the garden façade of the Palace *(above, left)*. Gushing a jet of water over 60 feet in the air, the fountain presents a sculptured group showing Apollo, the Sun God, driving his steeds through a foamy horde of whales, dolphins and Tritons. Sculptured by Jean-Baptiste Tuby, the figures are made of lead and were formerly gilded, like the ornate decorated post at left, which is from another fountain. An ingenious system of underground pipes, reservoirs and pumps feeds the fountains; Louis took great pride in these designs, which brought useful water to a place where there had been only a swamp.

Coypel: *God the Father in Glory*, ceiling fresco in the royal chapel, 1708

After the King's liaison with the pious Mme. de Maintenon, he and his architect Mansart made their last great contribution to Versailles—the chapel shown at left. The King wanted a church whose main floor could be used by courtiers and the public except on those days each year when he would receive Holy Communion. Above the richly marbled altar floor he wished Mansart to plan a gallery where he and Mme. de Maintenon could hear Mass in seclusion while the Royal Family and high nobility arrayed themselves beside the royal pew. To meet these requirements, Mansart was forced to design an unusually tall building. The interior, with its high colonnade resting on an arcade, is classically proportioned, but the décor is almost Baroque; white stone alternates with rich gold ornamentation on walls; chased locks, twined lily branches and the King's monogram brighten the doors; a violet marble banister circles the gallery.

The most purely Baroque element in the room is the ceiling, painted in fresco by Antoine Coypel in a dazzling display of *trompe-l'oeil* techniques; the vaulting, the stucco reliefs, everything is an illusion. Coypel's crowded scene, depicting the Eternal Father surrounded by angels carrying the instruments of the Passion, seems to burst through the roof from the celestial reaches beyond. Louis was thrilled with the work and is said to have come to watch Coypel paint every day.

In contrast with the colorful Baroque style that Coypel and others developed toward the end of Louis XIV's reign was the opposing tradition of classicism. Its chief model was Nicolas Poussin, France's greatest 17th Century painter, who was devoted to Greek and Roman antiquity and spent most of his life in Rome. A learned student of ancient art, history and mythology, Poussin sought his subjects in the classics and modeled his techniques on the principles of order, reason and truth that he discerned in the great works of the classical past.

The frantic scene at right, in which Roman soldiers are carrying away Sabine women to help populate their new city, is one of Poussin's masterpieces. The meticulous geometry of his composition, the careful drawing and modeling of the figures—caught at a peak of action—are characteristic of his best works.

Unfortunately, the rules and guidelines Poussin had evolved for himself were rigidly codified in the teachings of the Royal Academy, and many inferior imitators followed. But Poussin's example of a high moral tone, a methodically ordered and composed work, and the pursuit of truth inspired many great painters.

Poussin: *The Rape of the Sabine Women*, c. 1635

II

The Young Man from Flanders

If the Duc de Richelieu had not one day played tennis with Louis XIV, there is no telling how long the new century might have had to wait for the art that it yearned for: lighter in color and in spirit, less formal, less static. The Duke wagered his celebrated collection of paintings, built around Nicolas Poussin and the Carracci, on the outcome of the game. He lost. But collecting is an incurable disease; Richelieu, bereft of his collection, promptly started a new one by purchasing 14 Rubens canvases. All those who were tired of classicism rallied behind the great Flemish master of color, motion and light. Rubens' influence, combined with that of the Venetians and of Correggio, dominated and helped to define the artistic idiom of the incipient 18th Century.

Richelieu's artistic adviser was an argumentative critic, Roger de Piles, who engaged in a lengthy, complicated quarrel with the Academy. Pleasure, he asserted, in absolute contradiction to the official doctrine, was as important as instruction; color, the vehicle of the senses, mattered as much as line, the vehicle of ideas; Rubens, therefore, was a better model to follow than Poussin.

Because transitions are not always spectacular and memorable, we tend to think that the new art—usually referred to as French Rococo—was born overnight. Actually, its gestation was laborious. Like the new way of life for which it was to provide the setting, it developed at first away from, or on the margins of, court life. The agents were artists like Noël-Nicolas Coypel, Antoine Coypel and La Fosse who, trained under Le Brun and painting in his manner when working for Louis XIV, gave their imagination greater rein when working for his libertine nephew, the Regent-to-be, or for his rakish son, the Grand Dauphin.

Oddly, it was in the mansions of the King's own children and grandchildren that the new art first timidly blossomed. The old King himself relented and smiled when it came time to decorate a house for his grandson's child-wife, the 12-year-old Duchesse de Bourgogne, whom he adored. He found the proposed decorations too serious and decreed that the mansion be transformed into a doll's house for her. "There must be youthfulness in all that shall be done there," he declared. It was in this house, the Ménagerie—"a fabric of exquisite nothings," in Saint-Simon's wonderful phrase—that Venus and the amorous mythology which was soon to be the rage made their first appearance.

Unfortunately for Venus, these children and grandchildren died, and with them died what was left of the old King's capacity for joy. But the incipient artistic trend did not wilt away altogether. It sought refuge in private houses in Paris to which courtiers repaired discreetly whenever they wished to escape the chilling tedium of Versailles. It even found a paradoxical shelter in the domain of religion when Louis' regime restricted its commissions to that subject. Adam and Eve, Susanna and the Elders, Lot and his daughters were depicted with a frequency and in a manner that cannot be ascribed entirely to pious motives. Jean-Baptiste Santerre's picture of Saint Theresa, in the Chapel of Versailles, seemed so sensuous that priests avoided celebrating Mass in front of it; Antoine Coypel's angels, on the vault, look like cupids *(page 27)*.

Today, Coypel, Santerre, Raoux, Boullongne, La Fosse are little more than names. They felt the need of something new but for lack of personality were unable to define it. They had been the slaves of the Age of Louis XIV too long to know what to do with freedom when it came. They represent the unmaking of a style rather than the making of another. It would take a firmer hand to raise the curtain on the new age, to put away for good the cold, marmoreal presence of Louis XIV.

There is a celebrated picture of the 18th Century that today bears the title *Gersaint's Shop Sign (L'Enseigne de Gersaint) (pages 110-111)*. It depicts the premises of an art dealer where men and women dressed according to the new fashion are looking at paintings in the new taste. In a corner, a picture is being crated to be removed. The canvas is partly visible: it is a portrait of Louis XIV in the formal manner of Le Brun. The man who painted *Gersaint's Shop Sign*, and who thus unceremoniously packed away the Sun King, certainly did not intend to lend a symbolic overtone to the gesture, yet he had every right to do so, for he was the man who would give the century of elegance, pleasure and festivities its style. His name was Antoine Watteau.

The name of Watteau instantly conjures up the 18th Century, its quest of pleasure, its sociability and gaiety, its relentless pursuit of love. Yet Watteau himself was melancholy, retiring, and tasted of the joys of life, if at all, only sparingly. The diamond glitter of his pictures condenses all the brilliance of the age, yet his career remains shrouded in such obscurity that no more than five of his paintings can be dated with certainty. Indeed, the man who epitomizes the period of the Regency of Louis XV spent the better part of his career under Louis XIV and survived him by only six years: born on October 10, 1684, he died on July 18, 1721. The discrepancy is so great that one is tempted to think that a mischievous historian tampered with the records. But no, the dates are right, and, far from being confusing, they actually explain why Watteau was able to leave so perfect an image of the 18th Century. Nobody ever formed a clearer view of the Promised Land than Moses, who was not allowed to enter it.

Just as he barely managed to be a man of the 18th Century, Jean-

Antoine Watteau barely managed to be French. He was born in Valenciennes, a Flemish city conquered and annexed to France by Louis XIV, just a few years before the artist's birth. He was the second son of a master tiler. In a region ravaged by recurrent warfare between the King of France and his archenemy, William of Orange, the Stadtholder of Holland, there were plenty of roofs to be repaired: Watteau's father was prosperous. He was also violent. On one drunken occasion, he beat up a fellow citizen with a stick outside a tavern; on another, again after drinking, he broke a companion's leg.

Such a fellow could hardly be expected to look with favor on his frail and introspective son, especially when the latter—he may have been no more than 10 or 11 years old—announced his intention to desert the high profession of roofer for the humble one of painter.

As a result of Watteau's insistence, he was apprenticed to a local dauber, Jacques-Albert Gérin, whose rudimentary skills sufficed to meet the local demands for family portraits, pious pictures, carriage decorations and shop signs. How long he remained with Gérin we do not know: certainly no longer than was needed to realize that he could learn nothing from him. In about 1702, the youth ran off to Paris. His parents had long since ceased to finance his studies, even on a modest scale, and they let him go off penniless.

It was, as we have seen, the wrong time to be a painter—particularly if one had no money and no introductions. "Artists," wrote a contemporary, "earn their bread only when they have no teeth left." On arriving in Paris, the 17-year-old Watteau went to the quarter which to this day has remained a center of attraction for young artists with great hopes and small means: Saint-Germain-des-Prés. Being from Flanders, he joined the Flemish colony which had established its headquarters at *La Chasse,* an inn within sight of Saint-Germain's Romanesque spire. A fair was held periodically in the neighborhood, and the Flemish artists had secured the privilege of selling their paintings there.

His countrymen lost no time in informing Watteau that there was only one hope for a starving, novice painter: head for the Pont Notre-Dame. If a customer wanted a picture of his favorite saint, a scene of revelry, a fashion print or a copy of an old master, he was sure to find it at low cost in one of the dozens of art shops clustered on or around this bridge, which connected the two halves of the heart of Paris. Or he could order it, at minimum expense, from one of the many hacks who practiced their trade there.

Watteau found employment with one of the more successful of these manufacturers. If rightly forgotten as an artist, the man deserves to be remembered as a forerunner of the industrial engineer, for he practiced division of labor and assembly-line processes among his hirelings. One of them would paint faces; another, skies; still another, nothing but clothes; a fourth specialized in light-and-shade effects. Speedy execution was required. Three livres (French pounds) per week, plus soup, was the salary. It was the lowest rung on the artistic ladder.

Actually, Watteau stood a fraction of a rung above: he was allowed to paint his pictures from beginning to end. Among his specialties were a

Saint Nicholas and an old woman with spectacles, reading, by the Dutch genre painter, Gerard Đou. He knew the two pictures so well that he no longer needed to look at the originals to turn out his copies—a fact which enabled him one day to play a prank on the cantankerous wife of his employer. A customer had come in, asking for Dou's *Old Woman Reading*. "One Old Woman!"—or something of the kind—the dealer's wife may be imagined to have shouted in the direction of the attic where Watteau and his colleagues slaved. "Right away!" Watteau called back, but he did not come down to fetch the picture's original for copying, as he usually did. Impatience and worry gradually turned to anger in the lady's bosom, for she was afraid that such sloth might make her lose her client. In utter exasperation, she was about to go upstairs and give Watteau a piece of her mind when he appeared on the stairs and said: "The picture is practically finished, but I wonder whether I may have a quick look at the original to see exactly how the old woman wears her spectacles?" Rather than an expression of Watteau's high spirits, this innocent joke may well have been a protest against his fate, a pathetic expression of his despair at being a member of the artistic proletariat.

There was one compensation, however: the Pont Notre-Dame itself, lined with steeply gabled houses that made it look like an enormous saw. Together with its two neighbors, the Pont-au-Change, likewise covered with houses, and the Pont Neuf, it constituted the liveliest, most picturesque and most crowded quarter of Paris. Carriages, horsemen, pedestrians streamed endlessly from one bank to the other. To do so, they had to run a narrow, densely packed gauntlet of temptations. Clothes, sausages, boots, books, kerchiefs beckoned from shops and stalls. On the pavement, peddlers heaped melons, tomatoes, old cauldrons, and praised their wares at the top of their voices. Others wound their way through the crowd, chanting the street cries that were the sonorous signals of their trades. "*La vie! La vie!*" shouted the *eau-de-vie* merchant bent under the burden of her portable casket of brandy. "Here's health!" sang the watercress vendor. "Cream! Cream!" screamed a young woman who carried a bevy of milk pots on her head. Rabbit skins, pastries, matches, secondhand hats, oysters thus floated tantalizingly by. War invalids ambushed passers-by for alms, or offered a battered sword supposedly taken from a slain Turk. A man could also have his bellows mended, his knives sharpened, his teeth pulled. Indeed, eloquent quacks promised to cure anything from headaches to the pox.

To attract the attention of strollers, the men of pseudoscience often put on sideshows: acrobats, trained monkeys or marmots, and costumed dancers. Mountebanks performed slapstick comedies. And those who wished for more entertainment could watch the intense barge traffic, the quarrels of the washerwomen and the frolics of swimmers. Just off the bridges, there was the choice between the Place de Grève on the Right Bank, where executions took place, and the Foire Saint-Germain on the Left Bank. Here (as at the rival fair of Saint-Laurent), there were puppet shows, tightrope acts, card tricks galore. Gertrude Boon, known as "The Beautiful Twister," did her sword dance.

Every year brought a fresh contingent of freaks: the two-headed cow,

THE HERMITAGE, LENINGRAD

Gerard Dou's sentimental painting *Old Woman Reading* was such a popular favorite that it must have been copied thousands of times. The copyists, as was the practice in the 18th Century, were young artists grubbing out a living in Left Bank art shops. Watteau first made a living in Paris copying this picture. It was said that he became so familiar with it that he could paint it from memory.

a pigeon that would hop over a stick for the sake of the King, but would not budge when asked to do so for the Sultan. One year, the rhinoceros was *the* thing to see. Casanova relates how a gay party decided one afternoon to inspect this astonishing animal. A pretty marquise on whom he had his eye was particularly eager to see the wonder. "At the end of an alley sat a man who collected the fees," Casanova relates. "True, he wore African dress, was tan and colossally fat; nevertheless, he was of human and definitely masculine shape. The beautiful marquise went straight up to him and said: 'Sir, are you the rhinoceros?'"

Into this bedlam Watteau plunged at every opportunity, sketching the passers-by, the tradespeople, the judges and the beggars, the jugglers and the idlers, the thousand episodes of street life. Pad after pad was thus filled with quick, incisive drawings which Watteau carefully stored away —raw material to be used in better days when he would at last have the ability and the opportunity to paint pictures of his own.

But would those days ever come? In 1702 or 1703, an Academician would certainly have answered no. Watteau, who was born and received his first training in Valenciennes, undoubtedly considered himself a Flemish painter. And that, in his case, meant being a painter of genre pictures: down-to-earth, realistic renditions, modest in aspiration (and usually also in size), of the life of ordinary people at home and abroad, in town and in country. Solid, even heavy folk, who kept their houses clean but filled them with children and domestic animals, who worked hard but knew how to relax by indulging in equally solid pleasures: eating Gargantuan meals, drinking boisterously in taverns where the waitress would not be unduly outraged at an occasional pinch; stomping on the village square to the sound of bagpipes with a robust wench who without too much difficulty could be persuaded to retreat to a nearby barn or a haystack— such was the picture of life provided by the school of genre painting. Its Dutch branch handled these themes with more restraint and intimacy; its Flemish branch with greater lustiness. Both, however, can be traced back to the fleshy, popular works of Brueghel.

The aristocratic, idealistic class which dominated the France of Louis XIV, its imagination filled with the gods and heroes of "historical" painting, loathed this realistic genre art as much as it abhorred the burghers for whom it was conceived. Once the Sun King espied two genre pictures by David Teniers on a wall at Versailles. "Remove those ugly creatures!" he snapped. There was no room for them at the court, and all a practitioner of this style could expect was to eke out a meager livelihood by catering to the untitled people on the Pont Notre-Dame.

Yet the "ugly creatures" were finally to defeat the heroes and the gods. From the turn of the century onward, their vogue increased. Some time later, a nostalgic French critic bitterly complained about this invasion: "Pictures expressing great passions of the soul are replaced by low and coarse works without high thoughts, without dignity, without discrimination. A stable, a tavern, stultified smokers and topers, a cook with all the sordid instruments of her laboratory, a urinologist, a toothpuller: these are the subjects which today delight our connoisseurs."

The reason for this change is clear: absolute monarchy had gone bankrupt, the reins of power and of taste were gradually passing into the hands of the French bourgeoisie. Bourgeois Paris, not aristocratic Versailles, henceforth set the tone. Impoverished grandees married wealthy bankers' daughters. Louis XIV's mistresses had all been noblewomen: Louis XV's declared favorite, Mme. de Pompadour, was a commoner originally named Poisson. Clumsy, homely as they are, Watteau's earliest canvases—a cook, peasants dancing *(page 43)* or dining, a girl spinning, a boy showing a marmot—were, albeit unintentionally, on the side of the future: the style which he had inherited from his native environment was to become one of the major idioms of the 18th Century.

Watteau's first step toward freedom was his meeting, probably in 1703, with the painter Claude Gillot, who took him into his studio as an assistant. Gillot was a marginal artist, obscure like all of those who worked outside the sphere of court taste and royal patronage. In him survived some of the testy individualism of the Mannerist Age, which had been suppressed or brought under control by Le Brun. He was eccentric, brooding, susceptible—in short, very much like Watteau himself. Doubtless he would be forgotten today were it not for his contribution to the development of Watteau's talent. What he revealed to his young disciple was of priceless importance: that fiction could be as real as reality. For Gillot had a passion for the theater. He had designed sets for the Opera and managed a puppet theater. Actors and plays provided him with his favorite themes. He delighted particularly in depicting the characters of the *commedia dell'arte*—an Italian form of comedy based on standardized plot and characters and improvised dialogue—and he communicated his enthusiasm to Watteau.

The proverbial figures of the *commedia dell'arte,* imported by troops of Italian players, had long been familiar to Parisians. Warm applause greeted the antics of Pantalone, the ofttimes lecherous, miserly old man in the red pants and the long black cloak; the pedantic, ignorant Dottore with his black robe and doctoral bonnet; the obsequious, conniving Mezzetino in his silk suit with the bright red and white stripes; the gallant lovers Silvio and Leandro, the coquettish Colombina and Isabella, the dreamy, gullible Pierrot (also known as Gilles), white from head to toe, and of course the devilish, quicksilver Arlecchino, wearing a black mask, a checkered suit and literally quivering with stratagems.

Louis XIV himself had loved the Italians before Mme. de Maintenon converted him to austerity. He was particularly fond of Biancolelli, the star Harlequin. One day Biancolelli, present at the King's dinner, cast a longing glance at a course of succulent partridges served on gold plates. Louis XIV caught his gaze and ordered: "Give them to Harlequin." "What, the partridges too?" was Biancolelli's prompt reply. Another time, the King went to a performance incognito. When it was over, he complained to Biancolelli that the play was mediocre. "Don't tell it to the King," the actor whispered into his ear, "or he will fire me."

Fired the Italian players were in 1697—Watteau recorded the event in a painting now lost *(pages 50-51)*—at the request of Mme. de Maintenon, who could not bear their coarse gesticulation and salacious repartee a minute longer. But prohibition, as everybody knows, fans

Claude Gillot, the teacher who inspired Watteau's love for the theater, was so enamored of it himself that he often designed costumes and stage settings for comedies, ballet and opera. This detail from a Gillot drawing shows two popular *commedia dell'arte* characters.

desire. Bootleg *commedia dell'arte* now appeared at the fairs, in the guise of puppet shows, side shows, pantomimes or comic operas. Parisians welcomed these as a relief from, even as a protest against, the increasingly stately, motionless, rehearsed theater imposed by the classical age.

Gillot's paintings and even more his drawings reflect the *commedia dell'arte* spirit. His long-limbed, wiry, dynamic figures, taut and bouncy as metal springs, communicate with one another through staccato gestures and lightning dialogue. Watteau assimilated his master's style and subject matter so well that it is not always easy to tell them apart *(pages 44-45)*. It was the antidote the young painter needed against the ponderousness of his Flemish heritage. Gillot made him realize that the dream world of the stage was as good food for art as the real world of townsmen and villagers. He also revealed to him the virtues of leanness, of physical speed and of that mental counterpart of bodily alertness: wit. Of the latter, the Italians had so much that a French writer called the *commedia* a reservoir of salt.

But it was salt for the kitchen, not for the table. The Italians' jokes and antics easily lapsed into slapstick, even scurrilousness. The same was, in a way, true of Gillot: his compositions remain dry, jerky, brittle, popular. Perhaps this is what led to the two artists' brutal parting of ways in 1708, after four or five years of intimate collaboration. Both remained stubbornly silent about the motive of their quarrel. Gillot may well have been demoralized by his disciple's mastery, for he gave up painting and restricted himself to drawing and etching.

Watteau was, however, not yet ready to act as the spokesman of the century of elegance and refinement. He still lacked that indefinable blend of lightness, delicacy, exquisite manners and polished nonchalance known as *le bon ton*. Claude Audran III, his next employer, led him to the discovery of these qualities. Audran had succeeded Berain as France's foremost interior decorator. A decorator's talent consists in crystallizing the unexpressed aspirations of an age. Audran saw how the cumbersome, high hairdos and stiff bodices of Louis XIV's age were beginning to be discarded, how warm wood paneling and tapestries were replacing the cold formality of marble, how rooms grew smaller and more intimate.

Above all, Audran sensed the momentous revolution that was about to take place: women would set the tone. Caprice, playfulness, frivolity were becoming the fashion. A feminine curvaciousness started to soften the virile rigor of the classical setting; chairs and tables gradually assumed the sinuous shape of violins: the reign of the supple, sensuous arabesque had begun. Audran's brush made this intricate, interlaced pattern run in the borders of the tapestries, which he designed for the Gobelins, climb on the walls of drawing rooms and wind itself around gaily colored medallions where Chinese, monkeys, Harlequins and Columbines, shepherds and shepherdesses are reduced to charming disguises. Underneath, it is not difficult to recognize the elegant, artificial society of 18th Century Paris.

Audran's success was such that he needed assistants; among these, Watteau soon was the ablest *(page 46)*. In no time he assimilated the charming repertoire of pastorals and Chinese motifs and learned to waft

This sketch by Watteau of a wildly dancing couple is copied from a painting by Peter Paul Rubens called *Kermesse (Festival)*. Rubens' work, which Watteau studied at every opportunity, inspired him to seek freer and bolder expression in his use of color and in draftsmanship.

it deftly and lightly—as a lady powders her face—on doors, screens, harpsichords, fans. In later years, the basic pattern organizing his canvases appears again and again: the arabesque.

Audran lived and worked in the Palais du Luxembourg, of which he was the curator. This fact proved of great importance to Watteau's career, for it not only gave him access to one of Paris' most beautiful, least formal gardens but also to the series of 21 monumental canvases painted by Rubens for the Palace's builder and first occupant, Queen Marie de' Medici. The contact with Rubens' paintings was decisive: here was the treasure of which the genre painters whom Watteau emulated were merely the small change. The throbbing, pearly color, the transparency of paint that seemed impregnated with the imponderable aura which surrounds living people, allowed him to perceive the blood running beneath light skin; it lent to silk and satin garments such sensuous pliancy that they became yet another skin. These were lessons Watteau would never forget. Years later, when he was fatally ill, the Abbé de Noirterre sent him a small picture by Rubens. "From the moment I received it," Watteau wrote their mutual friend, Jean de Jullienne, "I have not been able to remain in peace and my eyes keep turning toward the lectern on which I have placed it as on an altar."

Rubens certainly has his share of responsibility for Watteau's rejection of the prosperous career which Audran held forth to him. It was the career of a decorator—the career which, to meet the worldly, frivolous demands of society, so many 18th Century artists were to follow. Watteau, however, was an individualist; he wanted to paint *his* world. He detested commissions. Sooner or later, his situation in the master decorator's workshop was bound to prove unbearable to him. Once he showed Audran an easel painting which he had done for his own pleasure: his employer advised him to give up this sort of work. Watteau instead resolved to give up Audran. In 1709, he entered the yearly competition held by the Academy, with the hope of winning and thereby gaining a trip to Rome. But he was beaten for first place by Antoine Grison—certainly the only occasion on which history has recorded that artist's name. Disappointed, Watteau resolved to return to Valenciennes. He had just sold his first picture, for 60 livres, to one Sirois, a dealer whose shop was on the Pont Notre-Dame. With that sum, he left Paris in 1709.

He sojourned in his native town for slightly less than a year. War was raging again in the northern provinces. Valenciennes teemed with soldiery, convoys, wounded men on convalescent leave. The gentle, delicate Watteau painted military scenes *(pages 48-49)*. Actually, this is not as surprising as it may seem, for the horrors of war are absent from Watteau's war pictures. Nowhere do we see shooting, blood, violence; the most dramatic episode in any of them is the explosion—at a safe distance—of a powder keg. Watteau's soldiers, more often than not, are busy resting or flirting. Nor was this an altogether erroneous picture of war as it was then waged. "Lace warfare," it has been called. In those civilized days, opposing army leaders maneuvered their troops like the figures in a game of chess. When one of them saw that he was about to be checkmated, he surrendered, and the superior officers of both camps would celebrate the event by having a good dinner together. Watteau's military scenes were thus only a by-product of his peaceful genre paintings.

And these were now beginning to sell in Paris. In 1710, therefore, he returned to the city and took up lodgings with Sirois, a gambling and drinking man who had buried one wife and was separated from another. Art dealing was a new but fast developing profession in France, still very loosely defined. Antoine Dieu, a business associate of Sirois, advertised his shop in these terms: "Frames, gilt and otherwise, bases for clocks and porcelains, crucifixes on velvet, vellum images, fish glue, stones of all kinds, and generally speaking every sort of works of sculpture, gilding, historical and decorative paintings—all for a reasonable price, retail or wholesale." Sirois himself frequently had trouble with the police, like many of his colleagues, because his declared profession—glazier—did not entitle him to sell paintings or even frames.

Watteau's choice of host was significant: throughout his life, he would remain outside the reach of the court and of official patronage. His acquaintances and friends were always to be art dealers like Sirois and his son-in-law, a man named Gersaint; rich collectors like Jean de Jullienne, dyemaker to the Gobelins; collectors and art critics like the Comte de Caylus or Antoine de la Roque.

Ten years had passed since Watteau first arrived in Paris, during which he had patiently accumulated the ingredients of his personal style. Ten years: compared to the swift rise of many painters of his stature, it was a slow, painstaking process of development. Simply keeping hunger at bay must have absorbed much of his energy. There is yet another explanation for Watteau's long search for himself: he had the ingredients—Flemish realism, Gillot's crisp theatricality, Audran's sinuous elegance—but had not yet discovered how to make the mixture jell.

But the time when he would was not far off. His sophistication was growing from canvas to canvas. A splendid barometer of this progressive refinement is furnished by the figures in his paintings, particularly the women. Women have always been clever at picking up the subtle winds of changing fashion. Follow those ungainly country girls who disembark in Paris from their native Brittany or Auvergne; observe how, with every passing month, they shed their provincial grossness, until the day when they possess that inimitable sparkle that makes foreigners exclaim at their sight: "How *chic,* those Parisiennes!"—and you have an exact equivalent of the transformation undergone by Watteau's female personages. The fat melts off them, they become slender and graceful, they learn how to dress, to walk and sit attractively, to cast knowing and witty glances, to signal with a fluttering fan, to appear more beautiful than they really are. After 10 years in the capital, Watteau's Flemish lasses have become Parisiennes.

The same process of Parisianization is evident in Watteau's style. The brownish monochrome inherited from the genre artists begins to glow wittily. Silvery light now ripples along the folds of silk dresses, flickers, scintillates, breaks and foams brightly on a cheekbone, a neck, a creased elbow or sleeve, as on the pebbles of a rushing brook. The figures become fewer and are assembled in subtler, more nonchalant combinations:

a mound swells up on what used to be a flat stage, and over its back the personages meander in graceful garlands. Indeed, landscape ceases to be a mere backdrop closing off the proscenium where the action takes place, and now responds to the same impulses as the figures: afternoon breezes echo the winds of passion.

Only a finishing touch was needed, now, for the miracle to occur. That touch, thought Watteau, only Rome could provide. Hoping to be sent there, he applied again, in 1712, for the Prix de Rome. In 1709 the Academy had thought him not good enough: now it thought him too good and instead of considering him as merely a candidate for Rome accepted him as an Academician. Once his "reception picture" was painted, Watteau would be officially received into the venerable company's bosom. But he would not go to Italy.

From the basement, Watteau, much to his disappointment, had been kicked upstairs to the drawing room. But the disappointment was short-lived. The influential Director of the Academy, Charles de La Fosse, had looked hard at the canvases submitted by Watteau and had become his ardent supporter. It is believed that La Fosse introduced his young colleague to Pierre Crozat, who not only patronized La Fosse, but gave the aging artist and his family shelter in his splendid mansion on the Rue de Richelieu. Crozat now made a similar offer to Watteau. His election had brought Watteau notoriety. Collectors, dealers, self-styled connoisseurs pestered him day in and day out. To escape from this new and, to him, unendurable excitement, he accepted Crozat's hospitality.

The brothers Crozat, Pierre and Antoine formed the vanguard of a new breed of men who were to be the masters of the age: bankers, speculators, publicans. The brothers came from a modest Toulouse family grown wealthy through commercial speculations. For the huge sum of 450,000 livres, Pierre bought the office of Treasurer of France, a highly fruitful investment. Although Voltaire jokingly called him "Crozat-Croesus," Parisians had nicknamed him "Crozat the Poor" to distinguish him from his brother "Crozat the Rich," whom the monopoly on trade with Louisiana had made even more fabulously wealthy. No longer merely the unpolished money-makers of the preceding century, these new financiers not only could afford culture but wanted it. Indeed, they often made it. The banker Helvétius, for instance, not only spent 300,000 livres per year on artists and writers but wrote one of the important philosophic treatises of the century: *On the Mind*.

Once a week, Pierre Crozat threw open his mansion to artists and writers. A discriminating as well as a generous patron of the arts, he welcomed those who wished to see his matchless collection, the pride of which were the portfolios containing some 19,000 drawings by the greatest masters: more than 300 by Rembrandt, 125 by Van Dyck, 100 by Veronese, 103 by Titian—a priceless hoard to which Watteau now had free access. And it was here that the miracle at last occurred.

Years later, speaking of Watteau, Eugène Delacroix said, "I was struck by the admirable artifice of his painting: Flanders and Venice are united in it." The Romantic Frenchman's diagnosis was absolutely correct. The authorities whom Watteau consulted most avidly were not

Raphael or the Carracci, as a 17th Century French artist would have, but Correggio, Veronese, Bassano and Titian—with the kindly La Fosse acting as mediator. Their works exalted color, atmosphere, the realm of the senses. It was a lesson that could easily be combined with that of Rubens—in fact, the great Flemish painter had learned from the Italians himself. But there was more. Behind Veronese, behind Titian, there hovered a presence which Watteau could not see but instinctively surmised: Giorgione, who had demonstrated, as no one had before, that figures and landscape could be brought into harmony and that this harmony was musical. Music was the really new and decisive revelation that Watteau received from Venice.

Music, too, permeated the atmosphere of the mansion on the Rue de Richelieu. Crozat loved music and patronized it. One of his permanent guests, La Fosse's niece, sang ravishingly. There were frequent concerts in Crozat's town house or at his country residence at Montmorency. He was the first Frenchman to prefer the Italian school of music to the French. Musicians, musical instruments, song, dance became the chief subject matter of Watteau's work.

It was these which led him on to the "admirable artifice" his work still required. Music provided the magic formula which enabled him to blend the disparate elements—music, and that of which it is the food: love. Through the latter, Watteau now attained the ultimate degree in refinement and polish. His contemporary, the playwright Marivaux, who was engaged in precisely the same process of filtering the grossness out of the *commedia dell'arte*, unwittingly described this miraculous transformation. Looking at a clumsy Harlequin, the Fairy Queen in one of Marivaux's plays says: "He is already the handsomest brunet in the world; but his mouth, his eyes, all his features shall be truly adorable once a little love shall have retouched them." The play is called *Harlequin Polished by Love*, a title that perfectly describes the development of Watteau's work. But whether music fosters love, or love music, one cannot say: as in Shakespeare and Mozart, they are one. Watteau's universe could equally well be termed a game of love or a musical comedy. In an unusual fit of inspiration, the members of the Academy, convened to pass judgment upon the pictures submitted by Watteau, coined a phrase that fits him so admirably that it has remained attached to his pictorial world: they dubbed him painter of *fêtes galantes*—an untranslatable term halfway between "elegant festivals" and "gay parties."

He was 30 years old. Within seven years, he would be dead. One is tempted to urge him: hurry up! And perhaps an inner voice was urging him just so, for he now entered on a period of intense activity. Painting after painting was instantly snatched up by eager collectors and dealers. So busy was Watteau that, despite the repeated warnings of the membership committee of the Academy, he kept putting off his reception picture. At last, in 1717, he delivered it. The Academy's patience could not have been rewarded more prodigally, for the painting, one of the few large-sized canvases executed by him *(pages 106-107)*, is the very quintessence of Watteau's poetic world of elegant fiction, musical sensibility and love: *A Pilgrimage to Cythera.*

The essence of Watteau's skill in drawing is his ability to catch the exact quality of a living gesture or attitude with the merest suggestion of lines. In the fragmentary sketch above, for example, only a few wispy strokes delineate the figure of a bass violist bowing his instrument. The classical preoccupation of the draftsman with three-dimensional form was of less concern to Watteau than the representation of the evanescent moment of human expression.

Ingredients of Grace

Two cultures, Flemish and French, plus many more subtle influences combined to inform Watteau's genius. Born and raised in a town that Flanders had ceded to France in 1678, he studied for a few years with a local artist who had been trained in the Flemish tradition. Watteau was preparing for a career as a painter of shop signs, tapestry designs, escutcheons for carriage doors and portraits for the local gentry. But there were pictures on the walls of nearby churches and in some wealthy homes that set the young man dreaming of a richer art than he knew from his uninspiring teacher. He probably saw some of the bold, colorful compositions of Rubens, and perhaps the glowing, gay genre scenes by many Flemish and Dutch minor masters, including David Teniers and Adriaen van Ostade.

At the age of 17, without money or so much as a spare pair of pants, Watteau trudged off to Paris. There, the bustling, sophisticated city life, the raucous comedy of the Italian theater, the music and dance of the street fairs broadened his personal experience and made deep impressions on his unformed art. The dancing peasants at right, probably painted during this period, show both the robust Flemish tradition he had known and traces of the graceful, more elegant French style he was learning. In time, through teachers, friends and the voracious appetite of his seeking eyes, he learned to express in paint an imaginative world whose sources lay in a great variety of places but were uniquely fused in his poetic vision.

The artist's Flemish background shows through strongly in this small work. The selection of peasant types as subjects and the almost monochromatic harmony place it in the Northern tradition of genre painting that goes all the way back to Brueghel.

Peasant Dance, c. 1702

43

In Paris, Watteau came to know many artists. One of them, Claude Gillot, a member of the Royal Academy who nevertheless managed to pursue a successful career outside the rigid categories of art as the Academy saw it, invited Watteau to become his apprentice. Accepting, the young artist made his first move away from the art of his past. Gillot had only a little in the way of technique to impart to his helper since he was not himself a very good painter. But he introduced Watteau to a subject that was to thrill and excite him artistically for the rest of his life:

Harlequin, Emperor in the Moon, c. 1704-1

44

the theater. Gillot especially loved the Italian *commedia dell'arte* players, and their irreverent wit and extravagant posturing also evidently appealed to Watteau. The brisk style of this improvisatory theater, its elements of fantasy and the actors' gifts of physical grace and expressive gesture became useful ingredients in Watteau's hands.

Both Gillot and Watteau painted many popular traditional scenes, and it is sometimes difficult to distinguish the work of the pupil from that of his master at this period: the painting at left below has been attributed to both Watteau and Gillot. The basic difference is that Gillot's style is rather more realistic, while Watteau's already shows the softer and more poetic treatment that will become his chief characteristic. Eventually, Watteau outstripped his teacher's skill and Gillot abandoned painting entirely, continuing only to draw and engrave the subjects which interested him. The two men parted after about five years of working together, but Watteau remained faithfully devoted to the theater for the rest of his life.

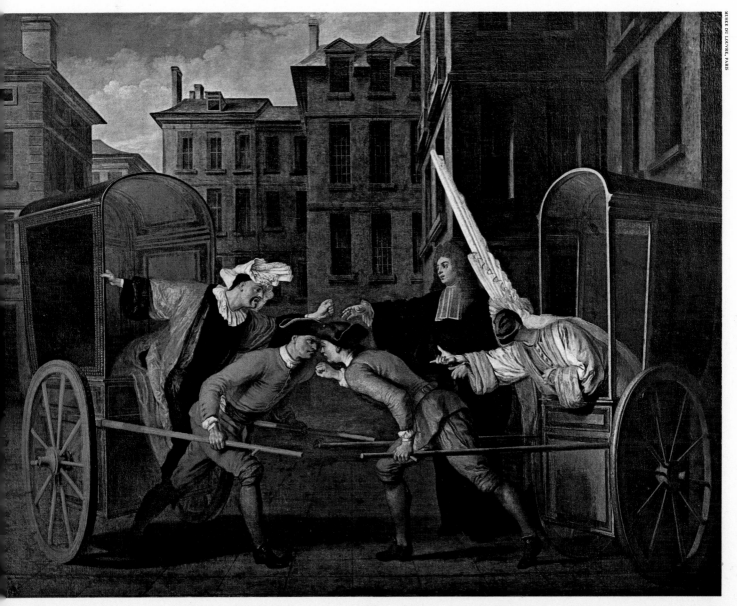

Gillot: *The Two Carriages* (a scene from the play *The Saint-Germain Fair*), c. 1707

WATTEAU

Audran: Two studies for decorative panels

T he third master to whom Watteau lent his talents
was Claude Audran III, the leading decorator in France.
Although Watteau's choice might seem inappropriate,
the decorator had more to offer than mere employment.
Audran's specialty was the arabesque, and the drawings
above indicate that no one knew better than he how
to weave and spin a line into a wonderful, frolicsome

creation. The finished wooden panel by Watteau at left
shows that the student caught the spirit of his master
well: monkeys in human dress cavort amid wonderful
curlicues of foliage, flowers and pure linear patterns, while
an amorous couple dances. From Audran, Watteau
acquired a sprightly, spontaneous feeling for design;
from there his imagination leaped forward freely.

tive panel, c. 1708-1709

In the summer of 1709 Watteau failed to win the Academy's prize trip to Rome and, disappointed, he left Paris to return home. Valenciennes was filled with soldiers, Louis XIV's troops having been swept back at Malplaquet. Although the fighting itself was fierce and bloody, the frequent stalemates enabled noncombatants like Watteau to wander among the encampments, where life, as the picture at right shows, was pretty much an easy routine. Watteau took the opportunity to sketch figures and groups and, during his stay, produced perhaps 10 paintings and many more drawings. The experience he gained in depicting figures in a landscape proved of great value when he began to paint his imaginative *fêtes galantes*.

INSTITUT NEERLANDAIS, PARIS, F. LUGT COLLECTION

Three recruits

MUSEUM BOYMANS-VAN BEUNINGEN, ROTTERDAM

Four soldiers and a woman

The Bivouac, 1710

49

Engraving by Tardieu: *Assis auprès de toy*, from *Recueil Jullienne*

Many of Watteau's paintings have been lost or destroyed due to the artist's often careless craftsmanship and the vicissitudes of time. Much present knowledge of his work, therefore, rests on a mammoth undertaking sponsored by his friend, Jean de Jullienne, a wealthy manufacturer of dyes used at the Gobelins tapestry factory. Jullienne engaged some of the best artists of the day to make engraved copies of Watteau's work, of which Jullienne owned some 40 paintings and 500 drawings. The engraving shown at right, from a long-lost painting, depicts the expulsion of the *commedia dell'arte* players from Paris by the aging, sanctimonious Louis XIV. Watteau had not witnessed the event but must have painted it because of his love for the Italian theater troupe.

M. de Jullienne shared with other important collectors of Watteau's art, Pierre Crozat and Antoine de La Roque, a great love for music and the other arts, and Watteau learned much from them. In the engraving above, commissioned by Jullienne after Watteau's death and perhaps based on lost paintings, the artist is pictured standing behind Jullienne, who plays the cello. Watteau's love for music, his understanding of its moods and rhythms, and his employment of musical themes and the atmosphere of music stem from his association with these cultured men of France.

Engraving by L. Jacob after Watteau: *Departure of the Italian Comedians in 1697*, from *Recueil Jullienne*

III

Painter of "Fêtes Galantes"

Paradises are easily lost, and the best way to lose them is to approach too close. They must be kept at a distance—remote—as Watteau managed to do in his *fêtes galantes*, those fragile confections that he so magically spun. The *fêtes galantes* are set apart. Their subjects seem far away, an illusion strengthened by the small size of the pictures themselves. And yet they are precise, like a stage viewed through inverted opera glasses. They are tiny enchanted parties, removed a great distance from the eye, and especially from the tough modern eye.

The particular paradise that we glimpse in Watteau's *fêtes galantes* is an island, a beautiful dreamy place that can be seen from the shore of everyday life. However, it can be reached only by ship—a ship such as the one he painted in his *Pilgrimage to Cythera (pages 106-107)*. But do not think that *anyone* may come aboard. This is a pleasure ship, not a ferryboat. If the smell of toil and worry hangs about you; if you are lacking in beauty, elegance or charm; if your mind has devoted itself, albeit fleetingly, to tasks other than the devising of love declarations you will never be allowed up the gangplank. Rather than expose yourself to the humiliation of being turned away, you will therefore be well advised to observe Watteau's exquisite creatures from the remote vantage point he has selected, for distance is the precise ingredient required in the recipe for translating reality into dream.

Watteau's dreamworld is not reality denied but reality transposed. You might even say transported—magical as fiction yet plausible as only fact can be. The elegant woman gathering roses in the second version of *Pilgrimage (pages 108-109)* has been lifted, down to the slightest detail in attitude and gesture, from an earlier drawing—but there she is a laundress with her apron spread out in her arms as if she were ready to hang out her wash. In many a servant girl slumbers the grace of a princess; Watteau knows how to awaken this hidden characteristic. And thus it is that everyday life, though it is not visible in his pictures, has had a hand in creating them. Those exquisite children, for instance, who tease a dog behind the backs of two bemused lovers—do they not evoke somehow a more familiar scene? Of course they do; we have probably just

The charming coquetry of this lady playing a lute—a companion work to a painting of a dancing youth—embodies the quality that the historians Edmond and Jules de Goncourt had in mind when they wrote that "the grace of Watteau is grace itself."

La Finette, c. 1716

seen it on our way to the museum, in the gardens of the Tuileries or of the Luxembourg (where Watteau strolled so often). It is *la petite bonne*—the little maid—who has brought her employers' children to play in the park but is so entranced by the compliments an enterprising soldier pays her that she has altogether forgotten about her little wards.

There is not a figure in Watteau's fairyland that is not based on sharp observation. The distance between reality and dream is precisely the distance between the drawings and the paintings. It takes time to traverse this distance; Watteau the draftsman reached maturity several years before Watteau the painter. That span is necessary for the magic to come into being, for the commonplace to undergo the sea-change which turns it into the rare.

What could be rarer, indeed, than the lovely gatherings which we espy in a clearing of the forest, at the turn of an alley in the park, near a statue or a pool, on a terrace leading out onto the gentlest of landscapes? Sometimes the gatherings form a rapt circle around a guitarist or a couple dancing a minuet. Always elegant, always graceful, the only activities tolerated are those in keeping with aristocratic idleness and leisure: picking roses and strewing them in a lady's lap, guessing who hides behind mask or fan, daydreaming, waiting for refreshments. Even the dogs lie lazily curled, and the children, impeccably brought up, indulge in genteel games. The atmosphere is like a crystal bowl which the slightest violence of gesture or of speech would break.

No danger of that, though; the actors of the *fêtes galantes* are mostly engaged in the difficult business of doing nothing. But how well they do it. One would never have imagined the variety of possibilities covered by that banal phrase: just standing around. Watteau's creatures stand, sit and lie about with a natural distinction and an effortless grace that could not be produced by years in a success school. They move with the natural poise of players from the Italian comedy and, indeed, those gay costumes are mixed with the refined fashions of the court. A civilization of peerless refinement achieves its climax in their gestures and attitudes. A cavalier leans on his elbow or bows to speak to a lady reclining on the grass; a young woman—there are no old ones in Watteau's festivities—turns her head slightly to listen to a remark by her neighbor; another accepts her paramour's hand to arise, or lightly rests her hand on his wrist to ascend a marble step. Another bashfully inclines her head at just the ideal angle that will show off, without seeming to, her swan's neck. To help a damsel disguised as Columbine decipher a difficult passage in a musical score, a gentleman dressed as Mezzetino brings his head just a trifle closer to hers than need be.

The sounds in Watteau's paintings are at once mysterious and dainty, like the confidential murmur one hears in a sea shell, the tinkle of two wineglasses, a lute tuning up, a guitar strumming with subdued vehemence, the bubbling of a fountain, the rustle of foliage, the whisperings of shy, young lovers.

For the supreme occupation of Watteau's parties is love. Always, there are multiples of two. Dance, music-making are mere pretexts or preludes; soon the gathering splits up into pairs and the great game of amorous persuasion and reticence begins. Every device of eloquence and seduction is employed by the men to overcome the ladies' hesitancy; treasures of wit are deployed by the latter to repel without offending —or to incite without inviting. They speak too softly and we are too far away to hear what they are saying; but fortunately Marivaux the playwright, Watteau's contemporary, was there and has recorded their golden banter. His elegant comedies show us the very same heroes—a mixture of *commedia dell'arte* players, conventional shepherds or peasants, and Parisians—flirting in the same gardens and parks.

To eavesdrop is bad: not to take advantage of somebody else's eavesdropping would be foolish. So let us listen to what Marivaux reports from behind the aromatic groves:

THE SHEPHERD: *You avoid me, beautiful Silvia!*

SILVIA: *What do you want me to do? You keep talking about a subject that bores me; you always speak to me of love.*

THE SHEPHERD: *I speak of what I feel.*

SILVIA: *Yes, but I feel nothing.*

THE SHEPHERD: *That is just what drives me to despair.*

In another part of the forest, the Marquis and the Countess are outbidding each other in artful timidity:

THE MARQUIS: *I should be so happy if Hortense were like you; I would be glad to marry her. As it is, I find it hard to do so.*

THE COUNTESS: *I well believe it; and it would be worse yet if you were to feel an inclination toward another person.*

THE MARQUIS: *That's just it: the "worse" has happened.*

THE COUNTESS: *What! You love someone else?*

THE MARQUIS: *With all my soul.*

THE COUNTESS (smiling): *I suspected as much, Marquis.*

THE MARQUIS: *And do you also suspect who the person is?*

THE COUNTESS: *No, but you will tell me.*

THE MARQUIS: *You would please me greatly if you were to guess her.*

THE COUNTESS: *Why force me to take the trouble when you are here?*

Through conversation, through the pauses in conversation which the lovers skilled in reading between the lines are quick to interpret, the love-war moves toward its expected conclusion. "No" and "maybe" give way to "yes":

THE KNIGHT: *Ah, Marquise, what will become of me?*

THE MARQUISE: *I blush, my dear Knight: what better answer could you wish?*

At this point, talk becomes superfluous, "it is too late," as one of Marivaux's cynical valets observes; "the hour for courage is past." Slowly, the pretty couples walk toward the shivering woods that proclaim in myriad whispers the burning desires which the lovers had not dared to voice, and disappear into the deep, protective shade. What happens behind the bushes we must resign ourselves not to see, but we can easily imagine it by looking at the marble fauns that tower above them. They blush. This curious phenomenon is less surprising than one might think, for Watteau's statues are so throbbing with life, so sensuous as to seem made of flesh. The once-over that the man in the left-hand corner

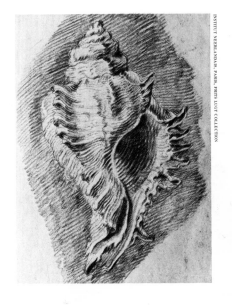

Watteau's drawing of a sea shell expresses more than an interest in nature; he was fascinated with the object's shape. And, indeed, the shell is a symbol of the style of the age; the Rococo. The word itself derives from the French word *rocaille*, meaning an ornament made of rocks and shells. Other characteristics of the Rococo style expressed in the shell are the irregular curves—arabesques —the asymmetry of the fronds and spikes and, less graphically, the phenomenon of growth and a sense of the exotic.

of *A Gathering Out-of-Doors (Réunion en Plein Air)* gives the pedestaled nymph hardly falls under the heading of art appreciation. Watteau himself did not draw the line very strictly: the stone goddess depicted in *Les Champs Elysées (pages 66-67)* is real flesh in the Louvre canvas named *Jupiter and Antiope (page 67)*. And after all, this is as it should be: love, as we learn from the story of Pygmalion, has the power to bring cold statues to life. Watteau's sculptures, stirred or driven down from their pedestals by desire, are the ultimate proof of the triumph of love celebrated in the *fêtes galantes*.

Slight, fragile, precious—what could be more perishable than Watteau's *Lesson of Love?* Yet, like those Japanese paper flowers, no larger than a fingernail, which unfold to many times their original size when dropped into a cup of tea, Watteau's tenuous *fêtes galantes* spread their influence across three quarters of a century. Indeed, practically all the dominant features of the age are to be found, prophetically concentrated, in his iridescent baubles.

What holds true for Watteau's settings is no less true for his actors. They influenced their time in a multitude of ways. The pink-and-gray, blue-and-yellow, violet-and-green harmonies in which he clad them—those marvelously delicate combinations that would be saccharine if they were not so precise—had a profound effect on the art, the interior decoration and the clothing of the age. Harlequin and Columbine, shepherd and shepherdess, step right out of his canvases to be duplicated in smooth glittering porcelain by manufacturers throughout Europe—at Meissen, Chelsea, Sèvres. From there they invade the fashionable interiors of the whole continent, from Naples to Stockholm. And as he filled his home with these delicate figurines, a man could recognize himself in them as perfectly as he could in the mirrors which now increasingly began to take up wall space, multiplying to infinity the sparkle of crystal chandeliers, gemmed swords, jewels and excited eyes.

The Italian *commedia dell'arte* players impressed not only Watteau and his teacher Claude Gillot but all of Europe. Scenes from traditional pieces and the familiar characters themselves found their way into tapestries, sculptures and designs for decorative objects. The figures above of Harlequin and Columbine dancing were designed by Johann Joachim Kändler for the Royal Porcelain Manufactory at Meissen, near Dresden in Germany.

Watteau invented the feminine fashion of the Regency, and it is only just that his name should have remained attached to a certain kind of pleat fanning out across the backs of ladies' dresses. But more basically he invented an entire attitude. He taught people, without their even knowing it, their exquisite manners, graces and looks. The figures in his *fêtes galantes* showed men and women how to sit, stand or walk with that mixture of sprightliness and nonchalance that is the hallmark of the 18th Century. They knew magnificence; Watteau taught them the meaning of elegance. They knew how to laugh; Watteau taught them to smile. One of the most popular novels of the Regency, the spicy *Persian Letters* that Montesquieu wrote before turning to more serious matters, describes the impressions of two Persian travelers in Paris. "The women of Persia are more beautiful than those of France," they reported home, "but those of France are prettier."

It was Watteau who taught women to prefer prettiness to beauty and men how to recognize and value the imponderables of which it was made: a new piquancy and glow, a new fire in the eye, a mobility and fineness of expression reflecting—as the Prince de Ligne, a superlative connoisseur of the gentler sex, put it—"the one hundred thousand things that happen in the upper part of a woman's face." Mobility and lightness, these flighty, playful, frivolous qualities, are summarized by an instrument that may be regarded as the very symbol of the century: the swing. And it is significant that we should see it introduced to the 18th Century in the painting of Watteau.

His overwhelming concern with merrymaking foreshadows the 18th Century's obsessive quest for distractions. "What efforts to make one party follow upon another and to prevent all accidents that might break them up," Montesquieu's Persian visitors noted about the Parisians. Anything was preferable to the horror of going to bed—to sleep, that is. "I fear I shall turn into a Chinese lantern," said the Prince de Ligne. "I have seen so many that I no longer know what night looks like."

Nor were festivities the dream of the aristocracy alone. Casanova, freshly arrived in Paris from Italy, was struck by the fact that "the Parisians loaf from morning to evening, finding amusement in everything." A military victory, the King's recovery from the smallpox, the birthday of a royal child, the visit of a foreign prince—practically anything served as a pretext for public celebrations. "The people in Paris talk only about festivities, about fireworks; great sums go up in powder and flares," wrote Voltaire. At one of these fireworks displays, several hundred thousand people jammed the Place de la Concorde; a panic occurred and dozens of onlookers were trampled to death.

At the triple marriage of Louis XV's grandsons, the guests of honor dined in the Opera House of Versailles, inaugurated on this occasion and transformed into a temporary banquet hall. Plates, cups, forks, knives, spoons—all were gold. From behind marble banisters, people watched the meal as one would watch a Broadway superproduction. In addition, the program included a state ball, theater performances, parades, ballets, fireworks. The Palace was illuminated at night and 160,000 Chinese lanterns hung from the trees; gondolas filled with musicians glided up and down the canal. A crowd of 200,000 Parisians gathered in the park saw the King appear on the balcony of the Hall of Mirrors, in a suit ablaze with hundreds of diamonds.

The favorite forms of entertainment were those, so treasured by Watteau, which best quenched the universal thirst for illusion and disguise: opera, the theater, and particularly masquerades, with their exciting atmosphere of incognito and intrigue. All France was stage-struck. Opéra-Comique, Comédie Française, Comédie Italienne played before full houses throughout the year. If, entering a country house or château, you found no sign of life, you could be sure that its inhabitants were busy studying their parts for the next amateur performance. When the scientist, philosopher and wit Fontenelle, in a treatise popularizing Newton's discoveries, wished to contrast the appearances of nature with the hidden laws that regulate it, a comparison at once came to his mind which everyone understood: the contrast between the glittering happenings on the Opera stage and the invisible manipulations backstage that made them possible.

"We are beaten and ruined, but Comic Opera consoles one for everything," Voltaire wrote at a somber turn in French history—in what might be described as a sarcastic mood if one did not know that he had actually built himself a private theater in his retreat at Ferney. The old philosopher would mercilessly press the members of his household and his guests into service as actors. When he was 81, he could still write from Ferney to his lifelong friend the Comte d'Argental, who was in Paris: "You are very lucky to be able to go to the theater."

To discover the cause of this furious passion for the theater, one need only consult Watteau's *fêtes galantes*. In them, actors, actresses, ladies and gentlemen are not only intermingled but indistinguishable. Indeed, the shepherd is, more likely than not, a lord in disguise and the princess is a player in stage costume. All the world's a stage, and never more so than when the world in question is that very special set known as *le monde*—society.

Eighteenth Century Parisians adored fetes and fireworks. Most popular were the "Venetian nights," which started with a water parade of decorated ships, sea monsters and floating stages, all lit by Chinese lanterns, and ended with a gigantic fireworks display that set the sky and the River Seine aglow. The one depicted here was held in 1739 under the walls of the Louvre to celebrate the marriage of Louise-Elizabeth of France and the Infante of Spain.

Society was perhaps not invented by the 18th Century, but it was certainly brought to a degree of perfection then that it had never known before and was never to know thereafter. "They say that man is a social animal," one of Montesquieu's astute Persians observed. "On that basis, it seems to me that a Frenchman is more human than anybody: he is man *par excellence*, for he seems made exclusively for social life." The latter exerted an almost hypnotic attraction. Every girl dreamed of marriage, not because of the attractions of a husband but because marriage brought access to society, to life in the plural. This is echoed in Watteau's *fêtes*; almost always they represent groups, not individuals. People regarded being alone with horror, as if it were tantamount to being buried alive. The unprecedented vogue of parties—"dinner parties are one of the four ends of life," said a lady of the time—is a symptom of the age's craving for company.

To hold your own in society, you had—then as now—to silence the individual in you, or at least to filter him, for thoughts and feelings too original threatened to rend the delicate social fabric. Sincerity, from the social point of view, is a form of rudeness. "But, Lisette," exclaims one of Marivaux's marquises who is comic precisely because she is outspoken, "is it possible to be sincere? The whole world is so polite!" To enter polite company meant to put on a mask, to play a part. All one's talent, all one's energy were devoted to playing it smoothly, to allowing no serious consideration, no sorrow—neither one's own nor another's—to interrupt the unfolding of the sparkling comedy.

The height of the social art was to make gestures and words perfected by years of patient rehearsal seem the fruit of improvisation, to lend conventional behavior the freshness of spontaneity. The glittering Rococo salon was the stage on which superlative actors, wearing silver wigs, dressed in silks of the rarest hues, performed with studied casualness the comedy of social life. If they cherished the theater so much, it was because they recognized in it the faithful counterpart of their own world, because its comedians were yet another mirror image—those mirrors with which they liked to surround themselves.

Of all the inventions of the 18th Century, the most breathtaking is that set of traits variously described as virtues or vices and covered by the expression "social graces." Refinement of manners had never been greater. Politeness had become second nature to the French. Every foreign visitor was struck by it. "'No' is not a French word," Casanova wrote admiringly; "instead of that disobliging syllable, say: 'I beg your pardon.'" On the battlefield of Fontenoy, French and British troops, neatly aligned, faced each other. "Shoot first, *Messieurs les Anglais*," said the French General with a bow, as if he were entreating a guest to precede him through the door. Such urbanity was the normal consequence of the first commandment of social life: to please. A book of the time bore the solemn title: *Essay on the Necessity and the Means to Please*. And it was no isolated case; all were thoroughly convinced of that necessity. Every gesture, every word, every attitude of Watteau's heroes and heroines is motivated by the desire to please. In fact, all his art reflects the epoch's imperative demand for amenity and categorically repudiates Poussin's dictates: ennoble truth, provide instruction.

This engraving, after a drawing by Augustin de Saint-Aubin, shows one of the thousands of *bals parés*, or dress balls, that were held in France during the 18th Century. The idea of the dress ball was born in France, and it spread all over Europe. With it went the dance called the minuet, which was the heart of each occasion. From the dance floors of Poitou, where it was invented, the slow and stately minuet flowed into the symphonies of Haydn and Mozart.

The foremost pastime was conversation. Never before, never after, have so many people talked so much, so continuously and so well. A man with a golden tongue was sure to find every house in Paris open to him; Casanova made a living, one might say, by relating his escape from the prisons of Venice. So much was dialogue regarded as the essence of human relations that when someone wished to say that a couple were making love the language of the day had it that they were "conversing." And when people parted—reluctantly—the conversation was prolonged by letters and by memoirs, of which the 18th Century produced many of the most entertaining in history.

This pre-eminence of conversation is quite natural, for it corresponds exactly to the ideals of society: it is as brilliant, frivolous, light and short-lived as the foam in a glass of champagne. Or rather, conversation could be all this, provided one had what was needed to sustain it: *esprit*—wit. The expression of wit is the witticism, and no epoch has yielded a richer harvest of these. They must be vivacious, seemingly effortless, swift as the thrust of a sword and as dangerously sharp. But wit has an invisible function which is no less important: to keep out of the conversation overly serious, dramatic, ugly or tasteless subjects. Wit must preserve the company's talk not only from dullness but also from those even greater perils: excessive intelligence and knowledge. For intelligence is the mind at work, whereas wit is the mind at play.

Witticisms are antidotes against unseemly exaggerations and insistence. By chance, Casanova meets Fontenelle, a feeble Frenchman nearly 100 years old. "I have come expressly from Italy in order to see you," says the Venetian, who did not shrink from a patent lie, particularly when he meant to flatter or boast. "Admit, Sir, that it has taken you a long time," Fontenelle replies with a barely perceptible smile. Such *bons mots* may be antidotes, too, against the unmannerly exaggerations of fate. The Maréchal de Boufflers had just been buried. "At least now I shall know where he spends his nights," says his wife. And with this remark, the grossness of death is reduced to the manageable proportions of a social event.

Wit was the goal of every Frenchman of the time, and a goal often attained, if we are to believe foreign visitors like Casanova, who called the French "the wittiest people in the world." Wit was an obsession.

The sudden and enormous vogue of coffee is partly explained by the fact that people believed it made the mind nimbler. If this is so, the personages of Watteau's parties assuredly must have swallowed cup upon cup before stepping onto the canvas.

What wit and conversation sought to demonstrate in a thousand glittering ways was the importance of not being earnest. "Trifling, which is naturally suited to sartorial matters," noted our Persian friends, "seems to have remodeled the general character of the nation: the French trifle at Cabinet meetings, at the head of an army, with an ambassador. The more seriously you practice a profession, the more ridiculous you appear. A physician would no longer seem grotesque if his clothes were less lugubrious and if he killed his patients triflingly." The importance of Watteau's dainty, frivolous *fêtes galantes* therefore cannot be overrated. It was not despite their being trifles, but *because* they were, that they played a decisive role. They gave artistic form and content to an attitude recommended by no less an authority than Voltaire, the philosopher who was the very incarnation of the spirit of the century. "Trifle with life," he said; "that is all it is good for."

Lightness of touch, the desire to please, good taste—all these were natural consequences of the first great revolution of the 18th Century: the triumph of woman. She was the center of every social circle, the arbiter of every elegance. Women made ministers, judges, even cardinals. "They form," Montesquieu's Persians remarked, "a kind of new state within the state." Their influence, the stronger for being subtle, took the bluntness off, and the heaviness out of, the French character stiffened by the virile ideals of Louis XIV's age. The 18th Century was, above all, graceful, and grace is a feminine quality. "Our continual commerce with women," explained Voltaire to his English friend Horace Walpole, "has introduced much more delicacy into our feelings, more propriety into our ways, more refinement into our taste."

Louis XIV had failed to conquer Europe; the dressmakers of the Rue Saint-Honoré succeeded. They set the taste in clothes for the entire continent. Every month two dolls dressed in the latest fashion were boxed and sent by the Rue Saint-Honoré to each of the leading courts. They were called Big Pandora and Little Pandora; the former wore formal, the latter informal dress. Not even war was allowed to interfere with the travels of these precious messengers of fashion: authorities everywhere doubtlessly had orders to let the couriers carrying them proceed unhindered. What Apollo and Mars had attempted in vain, Venus and Cupid thus achieved without effort.

Venus and her retinue of Cupids are familiar figures in Watteau's *fêtes galantes.* In the flesh or in stone effigy, the goddess of love is never very far away, while the winged cherubs flutter about the company like mosquitoes on a hot summer evening—a sure sign that every festivity must move toward a gallant culmination. In this respect, too, Watteau was the spokesman of the age. For love was the fuel which kept the social machinery going; it was the supreme weapon against Public Enemy Number One: boredom. "What can you do?" complains Clitandre, the protagonist of a contemporary comedy. "You are part of society, you are bored by it; you see women who are no more amused than you; you are young, vanity conspires with idleness. To possess a woman is not always a pleasure, but at least it is always a kind of occupation."

It need hardly be pointed out that this occupational love has little to do with the sentimental storm that threw Romeo and Juliet into each other's arms. Listen to Clitandre: "Never have people made less of a show of virtue. When two people feel a mutual inclination, they get together. When they become bored with each other, they part as casually as they got together. . . . Never do they quarrel. To be sure, love plays no part in all this; but what was this thing called love except a desire that people like to exaggerate, a movement of the senses that mankind in its vanity has chosen to call a virtue? Today we know that only inclination exists; and if we still tell each other that we are in love, it is not so much that we believe this, as that it is a more polite way to ask of each other that of which we feel the need."

In a word, love too must trifle. Passion is taboo, and if you are so unfortunate as to have really lost your heart, you must hide this disgrace. In amatory affairs as in all others, seriousness exposes you to the worst calamity that could befall you in society: ridicule. Show so much as a trace of jealousy, and all Paris will be laughing at you. Never have so many people had better reason to feel jealousy, yet shown so little. A husband who found his wife in a compromising position with her lover, exclaimed: "What carelessness, Madam! Just imagine what might have happened if someone other than I had found you!" For the one person you could under no circumstance love if you did not want to be branded an untutored provincial was your spouse. Marriage was one of those awkward necessities—like work—that could not always be avoided but that had to be tactfully ignored. A wife having expressed the incongruous wish that her husband spend the evening with her, drew this reply: "Husband and wife are one, and when I am alone, I am bored." It was a conservative retort, compared to the advice given by another husband to the young girl whom he had just married: "You must dissipate, my dear; that is the only way to give me pleasure."

François Marie Arouet de Voltaire, shown here in a bust portrait by Jean-Antoine Houdon, was a volatile curmudgeon whose voluminous writings kept all Europe stirred up for more than 60 years. His ideas and caustic wit got him beaten up by hired thugs once, exiled twice and jailed three times. He took sides on every public question, often changing his position and battling successive political regimes.

Pleasure was the alpha and the omega of life. "The philosopher is the person who refuses no pleasure," wrote Casanova, who, if this definition is correct, was certainly the greatest philosopher ever to have lived. No sociable soul would have thought of objecting. The Comtesse de Verrue, a lady who turned to collecting paintings with the same vivacity with which she painted the town red, explained that she had made her paradise in this world for safety's sake. In some ways, the France of that period was an earthly paradise. "It is a country made for young women and for men who cultivate pleasure," said Voltaire; "it is the country of madrigals and frills."

Those young women and men, those madrigals and frills, are they not the prime ingredients of the *fêtes galantes?* One is not surprised to learn that the "lady of voluptuousness," as the Comtesse de Verrue lucidly nicknamed herself, had several pictures by Watteau in her collection, for it is the entire 18th Century that enthusiastically embarked on his Cytherean vessel of pleasure.

The Rituals of Love

When Watteau was enrolled as a member of the Academy, his peers were hard put to describe his art. It fitted no conventional categories and the Academicians were forced to invent a designation. They called him a painter of *fêtes galantes.* Untranslatable into English, the term means roughly "elegant festivals" or "gay parties." In French, it also connotes far more—courtly love, social graces, tender romance; it thus perfectly describes Watteau's quiet, moving evocations of love.

But where had this withdrawn, unsociable man of provincial origins found the ingredients for such an art? The silk- and satin-bedecked figures shown at the right are not simply citified versions of the Flemish peasants *(page 43)* that he had painted in his early years. They are something more than that. They represent Watteau's discovery and exploration of a long and glorious artistic tradition. Before him, the Flemish master Brueghel had painted themes of festive love-making. Titian, the brilliant Venetian Renaissance colorist, had shown gods and goddesses dallying in secluded bowers. The great Rubens had created lusty Dionysiac revels and even the French classicist Poussin had painted the feastings of Bacchus.

Watteau came to know this heritage in the collections at the Palais du Luxembourg and in the homes of connoisseurs who befriended him. As he reached his maturity in painting he transformed the tradition into a unique creation. He invented the *fêtes galantes.*

In the never-never land of a *fête galante*, ladies and gentlemen play at the roles of shepherds, and turn from their flock to dance a courtly measure.

The Shepherds, c. 1716, detail

The Shepherds, c. 1716

The ingredients of Watteau's *fêtes galantes* are few: a park—the scenes are always set out of doors—a group of elegantly dressed men and women, a few children, perhaps a dog. Watteau blended these elements into art: adding a musical feeling of grace and harmony to the tradition of painting he had studied, Watteau turned into poetic picnics what other men depicted as orgies. In the process, it has been said, he created a purely French art: there were few precedents for such work in French painting. The tremulous leaves of his trees, his golden sunsets, are his own poetic invention. He had experienced the lush color of Rubens and the Venetians, and the draftsmanship of Audran and Gillot, but his colors and his linear style are his own. More than an observer of his society, more than a student of the past, Watteau used what his eyes showed him and what his mind told him, to create something beautifully new.

Gathering in a Park, c. 1716

A Halt During the Chase, 1720

Les Champs Elysées, c. 1718

Jupiter and Antiope, c. 1713

One of the most captivating elements in Watteau's *fêtes galantes* is the delicate balance he strikes between reality and illusion. In the two paintings shown here, the key to this interplay can be found in the figure on the pedestal at the far right in *Les Champs Elysées.* Is she a statue or a sleeping girl? Could it be Venus, dozing amid the charming revels in the scene below her? This juxtaposition of a statue and living people occurs in a number of Watteau's paintings. In one of them a gentleman is flirtatiously ogling a lissome stone beauty. But is she stone? Whatever the case, Watteau undoubtedly preferred to leave the answer ambiguous.

The painting above makes Watteau's thoughtful ambiguity somewhat clearer. Examined in isolation from *Les Champs Elysées* it seems only a beautifully painted mythological subject. But the sleeping nymph is identical with the statue in *Les Champs Elysées.* Watteau has breathed life so strongly into her that she transcends the myth from which he has taken her. The artist has been carried away by her beauty and the theme of love; he has painted a real girl lost in the warmth of a golden dream.

Dreams, reality, love—this is the stuff of Watteau's genius. Here the contrast between his art and his life becomes more than pathetic, for he never married and is not even known to have had a mistress. Before his death, he tried to destroy the nudes he had painted. Whatever late piety led him to that action, future generations are fortunate that he did not live to carry out fully his attempted absolution.

67

Love in the French Theater, c. 1714

Love in the Italian Theater, c. 1714

Fêtes Vénitiennes, c. 1719

The theater had fascinated Watteau since his early days in the studio of Gillot. He often pictured actors, sometimes mingling them in his scenes with the elegant participants of *fêtes galantes,* and he delighted always in the theater's juxtaposition of reality and illusion. In one instance, he plays a trick on the theater by picturing a night scene *(lower left)* in full darkness. Actors usually performed in full daylight, creating the illusion of darkness with candles or by verbal references, but Watteau has made their illusion real.

Some of Watteau's friends appear in the guise of actors in the theater paintings. The portly painter Nicolas Vleughels is shown dancing in *Fêtes Vénitiennes,* perhaps a scene from a ballet presented at the Opéra.

69

Much as he appreciated actors and clowns —the children of the theater—Watteau had an equal enthusiasm for children, many of whom he portrayed in his group scenes. Indeed, few of the *fêtes galantes* shown on the preceding pages are without a child or two. In his pictures they shine with bright-eyed innocence, the rosy-cheeked expectation of youth. Thus, they provide for him a poetic image that still further carries the *fêtes galantes* into the realm of fantasy. These are not rowdy urchins, mischievous imps or hoop-rolling caricatures of children that a genre painter would have included to get a laugh or to evoke a wistful smile. Watteau's children are scaled-down versions of the men and women who populate his love plays, and like those gentle individuals they remain shielded in his world from the ravaging age lines of reality. Like their parents, they are timeless, rare creatures for whom the clock stands still.

In *The Dance,* shown here, Watteau devoted himself to a child's world. The youngsters are engaged in that typical activity of childhood, imitation. A boy takes the musician's role; one of the girls prepares to show her steps. Watteau is fascinated with their earnestness, the eager and complete concentration with which they throw themselves into their parts. Each child's focus is inward; they are totally absorbed. And this quality, especially in this impressive painting, is what interested Watteau most. Like the participants of the *fêtes galantes*, these children are in a dream.

Comparisons have been made between the monumental figure in this work—the little girl —and the character with which Watteau seems to have identified himself most closely, Gilles. In those later paintings of the sad clown *(pages 112 and 113),* that larger-than-life figure forces his isolation, his otherworldly spirit out of the painting into the viewer's consciousness. Here the little girl is projected in the same fashion, as a dreamed image of womanhood, of beauty and, in Watteau's magical portrayal, of life.

The Dance, c. 1719

The Music Party, c. 17

The Music Lesson, c. 1717

Watteau frequently repeated subjects in his paintings, and even more often he used particular figures more than once, as the pictures on these pages show. It was no lack of invention that led him to this device but rather, one supposes, a confident use of images that he found satisfactory. He may have felt no need to re-invent once he had devised a figure whose expression, gesture and attitude said as much as it should. Thereafter, he could be certain that each character would convey his meaning. Thus, he developed a repertoire of familiar figures that he used in a variety of compositions.

The lute player in *The Music Party* *(above)* is used almost without variation in *The Music Lesson (left)*. On the opposite page the works at top contain a pair of repetitions shown in detail below.

Fêtes Vénitiennes, c. 1719, details below   *Gathering in a Park,* c. 1716, details below

The details at left from the paintings above show how Watteau repeated a bit of amorous play between two members of outdoor parties. In addition, the bagpiper on the right side of *Fêtes Vénitiennes* also appears in the painting on page 64 titled *The Shepherds.*

Here Watteau repeats the figure of a seated woman, reproducing with only the slightest modifications virtually every fold of her gown and each highlight on the silken cloth.

73

Harlequin and Columbine, c. 1714

Lancret: *Italian Comedians by a Fountain*

Although Watteau was able to repeat himself successfully a number of times, his delicate touch and atmospheric moods proved incapable of convincing imitation. Of the artists who attempted to work in his style, one of the most successful was Nicolas Lancret, whom he had met in Gillot's studio, where Lancret was enrolled. Like Watteau, Lancret took from Gillot an appetite for the theater, which he satisfied in paintings such as the one above. But although it is a charming work, well painted and with an authentic spirit of *fête galante*,

Lancret's lack of invention is betrayed by a comparison with Watteau's painting, shown at left; the two main figures in Lancret's scene have been lifted almost directly out of Watteau's with a few minor changes.

In other works, however, Lancret showed greater originality while remaining essentially a painter of *fêtes galantes*. Unlike Watteau, Lancret was favored with a number of official commissions, painting several works for the royal apartments at Versailles. At his death, in 1745, the *fêtes galantes* tradition came to an end.

75

The only pupil Watteau is known ever to have accepted was Jean-Baptiste Pater, who was 11 years his junior and came from Valenciennes. But their association did not last long. Gersaint, the art dealer, explained that "Pater found a master who was too temperamental and too impatient to be able to put up with the weakness of . . . a pupil."

Watteau's art was not a matter of techniques to be learned, nor was his spirit one that could be imparted. As this picture of bathers shows, Pater was much more explicit in his love scenes than Watteau ever was. Pater overstated what his master had only whispered. He parted curtains that Watteau would never have drawn. The nudity, the unveiled eroticism of this scene, and the many that Pater followed it with, would have been unthinkable for Watteau.

Nevertheless, Pater's scenes are charming compositions and they became extremely popular. He achieved a good career, if only by partly trading on his teacher's great fame, and many of his pictures were mistaken for those of Watteau.

Pater: *A Bathing Party in a Park*

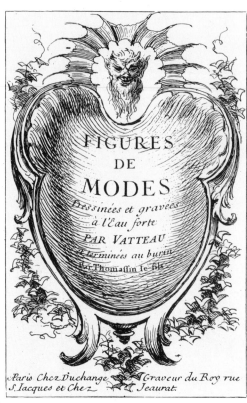

FIGURES
DE
MODES

Dessinées et gravées
à l'Eau forte
PAR VATTEAU
et terminées au burin
Par Thomassin le fils

Paris Chez Duchange   Graveur du Roy rue
S. Iacques et Chez   Jeaurat.

IV

Capturing the
Golden Moment

In the aftermath of the 17th Century, Watteau invented the language through which the 18th Century was going to express itself. He made Rubens operational once again by miniaturizing his grand manner. He substituted elegance for majesty, and wit for weight, and forced dark, stiff solemnity to give way to light colors and sprightly brushwork. France was tired of heroics. Watteau taught French painting to smile and to dance. He sensed that the modest scale and familiar approach of genre painting coincided with the aspirations of the new age; and he showed how this unpretentious framework, previously used only to depict pedestrian reality, was equally suited to the representation of fantasy, poetic dream, even mythology.

Watteau thus provides the earliest and most perfect incarnation of Regency tastes. In many ways, this was a dubious privilege, for within 50 years the age and its artistic production were to be scoffed at and rejected. Watteau himself, however—or at least his reputation—would gradually recover from the condescension and contempt showered on the Regency period by later epochs. Gradually it would become evident that his paintings were not just period pieces. Increasingly it became clear that there was something that made Watteau different; we must try to define that something, for it is the essence of his work.

The difference can be measured by comparing Watteau's *fêtes galantes* with those that apparently resemble them most: those by Lancret, who was apprenticed in the workshop of Gillot after Watteau had left, and by Pater, who, as a native of Valenciennes, had naturally come to Watteau for lessons. Both painted so much in the master's manner that scores of pictures by them have long been attributed to him. A superficial resemblance does exist between them, but the resemblance is that of a cultured pearl to a natural pearl.

The difference is that Lancret and Pater do too much. They make explicit what Watteau leaves implicit. The scent of love floats the more effectively over Watteau's pictures for its not being flaunted. Practically no kissing, no embracing occurs in them. The theme of the *fêtes galantes* —which harks back, through Rubens, through Poussin, to the baccha-

In the last years of Louis XIV's reign, the rising middle classes became interested in fashion, and artists catered to the vogue. Watteau made these etchings of the clothing of his day but, unlike other engravers, he failed to catch the public fancy with such pictures.

Fashion Figures, c. 1710

nalia of Titian—is toned down till only the presence of a bottle of wine in a corner or a glass in someone's hand reminds us of their boisterous origins. But nobody is ever seen drinking. Watteau's personages never forsake their discretion and reserve. His license is purely poetic.

The figures represented by Pater and Lancret display no such restraint. They would not think of refraining from kissing and clasping in public. Nor does the wine remain in its bottle; it flows freely, food is spread on the grass, and quickly the elegiac gathering turns into an indubitably merry but prosaic picnic. One more draft of claret, and it may turn into an orgy—it often *does,* for neither Lancret nor Pater would want to stop on so tempting a way. They insidiously invite us to the visual exploration of reclining damsels' legs or to a hiding place in the bushes to watch them bathe, as in the painting shown on pages 76 and 77. In Watteau's pictures, the curtain invariably falls before the women.

But the poetry-generating distance that the master always preserved cannot prevail against the insistent curiosity of his disciples. We are eye-witnesses when, in Lancret's *Morning,* a bare-bosomed beauty serves coffee to a very worldly *abbé* for whom her charms obviously hold no more secrets. The absence of secrets, of mystery is what distinguishes the imitators from their model. As the phrase has it, Lancret and Pater put the dots on Watteau's i's. Spicy reality replaces immaterial dream; tender poetry yields to naughty narrative. It is no coincidence that Pater turned *The Comic Novel,* a salacious, picaresque tale by Scarron, into a sequence of small canvases that might be defined as a comic strip in paint. One can easily imagine how well it must have been received.

Watteau's works do not narrate. It is true that they often seem to represent scenes from a play; from what play is usually impossible to determine. Even in a farcical episode like his *What have I done, ye cursed murderers,* borrowed from Molière, in which a foolish country squire is threatened by a mock-physician with an enema of colossal proportions, the majority of the actors seem unconcerned. This strange indifference of Watteau's personages to the action in which they are supposedly engaged puzzled and irritated even his supporters. "His compositions have no object. They express the manifestation of no passion and hence are lacking in one of the most fetching parts of painting; I mean action," Watteau's friend, the Comte de Caylus, writes petulantly. So wrapped in mystery, so uncommunicative is his subject matter that *A Pilgrimage to Cythera*—that famous picture which for the past 200 years had been understood as a sailing *for* Cythera—has recently been interpreted as a sailing *from* Cythera!

Let us look again at Watteau's *fêtes galantes.* We have described them as amorous banter; yet barely a gesture is ventured, not a word is heard. The artist may have intended at the outset to tell a story, but the anecdote is hushed by the emotional distance. Conversation, dance, song are magically suspended. A strange, golden silence holds everything and everyone under its spell. And this silence leads us to reconsider more attentively the heroes and heroines of Watteau's parties. They are not as joyous as we had thought they were, but to say that they are sad would be going too far. They appear not to believe in their happiness. They

Strongly reminiscent of Watteau's style is this drawing by Nicolas Lancret. Like Watteau, Lancret began by studying with Gillot. When Watteau met Lancret he urged him to stop imitating Gillot and to draw directly from nature. Instead, Lancret took to imitating Watteau, and he did it so effectively that his work was often taken for the master's. This so mortified Watteau that he broke off their friendship.

seem curiously uninvolved, as if listening less to a sweetheart than to an invisible, pressing interlocutor, a voice from within. In the message of that voice lies the secret of Watteau.

The key to it is music, whose implements occur so frequently in Watteau's canvases—the guitars, lutes, mandolins, violins and cellos, the scores interpreted by singers and dancers. Indeed, even one of the earliest known pictures by the artist, *La Marmotte*, strikes up the theme of music, albeit in a humble, homely way. Significantly, Watteau discovered his style at the same time that he discovered the world of music, which opened itself to him in Crozat's mansion in the twofold guise of concerts and the music-oriented paintings of the Venetians.

What we took for unconcern on the part of Watteau's personages is really intense concentration. Somewhere around them or inside them a grace note is being sounded which they must catch if their love—and if the picture—is to attain perfection. At times the canvas has the indecision of an orchestra tuning up; at others, it has the nostalgic, lingering quality one experiences when the music has ceased and resonance melts into recollection. Sometimes, as in *The Concert* or *The Music Party (page 72)*, the note is caught and held by all, from the lute player who strikes it to the distant trees that echo it.

Jean-Baptiste Pater, who drew this man with a pipe, came from Valenciennes and for a brief time was Watteau's pupil in Paris. Like Lancret, Pater became a skilled imitator of Watteau's style after he left the master's studio. During the last months of his life, perhaps feeling the need to leave an artistic heir, Watteau sent for Pater and generously gave him both instruction and some unfinished work to complete.

Music had often furnished themes for painting. But here it does something more; it provides the composition. With their long, straight, svelte bodies and their small, tilted, oval heads, the figures are disposed in such a way that they almost look like transpositions in paint of a few bars of musical notes from a suite by Rameau or an air from an opera by Campra. Music alone provides a clue to the painter's compositions. There are only a few notes in music, but their combinations are infinite. Similarly, Watteau again and again uses certain figures from his drawings, but combines them in endless variety. Every figure is sharp and precise, yet the composition as a whole is like a shimmering, indefinable fabric, just as individual notes blend into a harmonious score. The intervals that separate the figures, furthermore, are musical intervals, active silences skillfully introduced into the composition to highlight the sounding of isolated or grouped figures. And the personages, a-glitter with light or color, are related to the muted, uniform, brown-green background of foliage as soloists are to choir and to orchestra. Never before, not even in Giorgione's Venice, had music played so vital a part in the work of a painter.

And this tells us something essential about Watteau. For the raw material of music is time, just as the material of painting is space. Painting seizes upon a temporal event—historical, mythological, religious—and immobilizes it within the space of a picture. Watteau reverses the process. He paints musically, temporally. It is not merely a matter of representing time as an old man with a sickle or as a woman with an hourglass; such allegories abound in the work of Watteau's contemporaries and predecessors. With Watteau, time becomes an integral part of the fabric of the work. An early picture, *The Recruit Going to Join the Regiment*, apparently shows a number of military figures—but only apparently, for what it really shows is one figure in a succession of attitudes. In a word, it strives to achieve an effect not unlike that of the most temporal of all art forms, the cinema. Had Watteau resorted to this unusual method only once, one might have attributed the experiment to chance or to idle curiosity. But he does so again in one of his supreme masterpieces, the picture that epitomizes the universe of the *fêtes galantes: A Pilgrimage to Cythera (pages 106-107).*

At first sight, the cast is composed of a dozen or so pairs of lovers in different attitudes and attire. Yet there is a strange similarity in all the men's heads, and in all the women's. No wonder; what we are really being shown is one couple at various moments of a rapturous afternoon. As we read the picture from right to left, we follow the love-pilgrims' progress toward the ship that will carry them away. The lovers arise; next they walk off; at last they board ship. Watteau clearly wants us to read the picture in this filmlike manner, with the action winding its way, first crescendo, then decrescendo, over the gently rolling back of a small mound of earth. The glances cast forward and backward by the lovers provide glissando transitions between the successive phases of what is clearly a metaphorical account of the rise and decline of a love affair.

While *Pilgrimage* offers the most systematic utilization of temporal devices, they are to be seen in some form in most of Watteau's works. His personages are always either coming or going, ascending or descending that gentle swell of earth, one of his favorite props; and when they are resting, they are echoed in the remote distance by ethereal figures who look less like real people than like diaphanous ghosts occupying the spot where their more material counterparts are already in spirit or shall soon be in body. Everything, in short, speaks of passing—in other words, of time.

Watteau's awareness and use of time make his art especially appropriate today, since nothing characterizes the modern age so much as a concern with progress. And progress is change, a transformation in time. But Watteau could have introduced his esthetic revolution at no other moment in history. For the incipient 18th Century really discovered time. Historical consciousness, the sense of relativity, the belief in progress—all these signs of the awareness of time and of its passing have their roots in the early years of the century. Time is born out of the disintegration of eternity; it was thus natural that an intense feeling for time should spring up in the shambles of a regime which men—or at least Frenchmen—had become convinced was immortal: the absolute monarchy of Louis XIV, the Sun King.

Now all seemed plunged into flux, change and restlessness. Yesterday's ally was tomorrow's foe; a valet on Monday became, through speculation, a financier on Wednesday; a banknote was worth gold at dawn and dust at sunset. The age was discovering a manifestation of passing time still very much with us today: the news. When a Parisian wished to hear fresh news—real or imaginary—all he had to do was to go to the Tuileries Gardens, in front of the Louvre, and station himself near the bench where a new species of people, the *nouvellistes,* had their appointed meeting place. The *nouvellistes* devoted their lives to the collecting, inventing and spreading of information. The fact that the next day usually proved them wrong did not detract from the authority and con-

A smiling, self-confident young Savoyard, or street musician, with his fipple flute and tame woodchuck attracted Watteau, who made this sketch. All the standard street characters of Paris—and especially the musicians—appear in Watteau's sketches. This flutist was later pictured in a full-scale painting called *La Marmotte.*

tinued attraction of these oracles, their listeners' ability to forget yesterday's news being at least equal to their eagerness to learn today's. In a word, they were newspapers in the flesh. And newspapers in the more portable form known nowadays also were beginning to prosper.

In this climate of inconstancy and instability the principles of permanent beauty that Poussin and Le Brun believed they had set up securely forever suddenly seemed no more absolute than all the rest; they became a mere passing expression of a passing taste.

Of course, this was not the first change to occur in art. Up to then, however, changes had always been followed by long periods of stability, and although they often caused violent uproar and protests, the ensuing calm gave everyone ample time to assimilate novelties. In the end, people forgot that these changes had only been expressions of relative tastes, and worshiped them as if they were absolute laws. The new thing, therefore, was the acceleration of change. The wind of time began to turn the pages of history's book with such speed that people no longer had the leisure to learn its contents by heart. One taste gave way to another before it had time to rise to the status of a law.

The most spectacular manifestation of this accelerated pace of time was an altogether new phenomenon, soon to exert on France a tyranny so implacable that not even Louis XIV would have dared to dream it: fashion. "The divinities worshiped here, though no altars are raised to them, are novelty and fashion," wrote Casanova. Parisians succumbed to one fad with an ease equaled only by the facility with which they fell prey to the next. One day, Louis XV, who had been hunting, stopped by chance at a dismal inn near Neuilly in the suburbs of Paris and asked for a glass of liqueur which he pronounced good; instantly, the inn became fashionable and the owner, grown prosperous in a few months, built himself a superb house bearing the proud, and appropriate, inscription: "Out of liquid, solid."

All eyes, it seemed, were focused on the tastes of the nobility—and they became aware of their power. Wishing to be of service to a young protégée who had just married and opened a tobacco shop, the Duchesse de Chartres decided that the best way was to stop her carriage ostentatiously in front of the establishment and to buy her snuff there. Her guess proved correct. After she had stopped there three times, the shop became the rage; no one in Paris would have dreamed of buying his tobacco anywhere else; wealth was the young woman's wedding gift.

The area where fickle, capricious fashion held sway most despotically was dress. As early as 1716, a chronicler noted: "Our parents' garments seem like disguises to us." Last week began to seem ages ago; in chattering to his customers a well-known hairdresser of the time gave up the word "yesterday" and substituted "formerly." The process of acceleration terrified Montesquieu's two fictional Persian letter writers. "You wouldn't believe," one reported home, "how much it costs a husband to keep his wife fashionable. A woman who leaves Paris to spend six months in the country returns looking as antiquated as if she had spent 30 years there. A son does not recognize his mother's portrait, so alien does the dress she wears in it appear to him; he fancies that it rep-

The soaring spirits of the early 18th Century were reflected in the fashionably rising heights of ladies' hats and hair styles. The collection of feathers, flowers, fancy ribbons and ornaments above was but one of 200 voguish creations on sale in one Paris season. The unwieldy hairdo caricatured below caused its chic but top-heavy wearer to kneel in her coach with her head out the window when she went for a drive.

resents some American woman, or that the artist wanted to paint an imaginary lady. Sometimes, hairdos grow gradually taller till a revolution brings them down again in one fell blow. There was a time when their immense height made a woman's face appear to be the middle of her person; next, it was the feet which seemed to occupy that central position, for the heels composed a pedestal which raised her high in the air. Who could believe it? Architects have often been forced to raise, to lower and to widen doors according to whether women's accoutrements required such changes."

This being the century of woman, and woman being particularly receptive to fashion, its tyranny exceeded all bounds. There exists no better testimonial to its power than the fabulous conceit that was displayed by dressmakers and hairdressers. Rose Bertin, dressmaker to Queen Marie-Antoinette, was rightly called "the Minister of Fashion" and behaved like one. Haughty, contemptuous, she could brook no contradiction. When a lady customer failed to express delirious enthusiasm for what was shown her, *la Bertin* snapped: "Show Madame samples of my latest collaboration with Her Majesty." To a gentleman who had dared to complain about her exorbitant prices, she replied: "Does Vernet [one of the most expensive painters of the time, whom we shall meet again later] get paid only for his canvas and for his pigments?" Slaves make the master. Had women—and men—not groveled at their feet, would the grubby caterers to fashion ever have thought themselves the lords of the world? Would Charpentier, the *à la mode* bootmaker, have been able to invite noble customers to dine with him, casually adding: "We shall put on *Oedipus* after dinner"?

In fashion, only the old and the familiar are ridiculous. The tastemakers of the 18th Century outdid themselves in the inventing of novelties. Gowns were dyed in unheard-of shades enticingly dubbed "blushing nymph's thigh," "Paris mud," and "Queen's hair," the latter after one of Marie-Antoinette's pale golden locks, which had been sent to Lyons for the dyers to copy and had become very popular. Anything new, anything unfamiliar could serve as inspiration. There were trimmings *"du système"* in honor of John Law's introduction of the paper money system, toilet articles *"à la comète"* to commemorate the celestial body identified by Halley, and dresses *"au rhinocéros"* inspired by the famous animal exhibited at the fair of Saint-Germain.

War, calamities, discoveries, the day's celebrities—the thousand and one events, great and small, of which history is made—thus found their ultimate destination in fashion. Bonnets were named *"à la débâcle"* (French for the thawing of ice) when the frozen Seine had begun to melt; *"à la révolte"* when the populace rioted to demand bread; an inflated one was of course named *"à la Montgolfier,"* after the brothers who had just soared skyward in their balloon.

But the greatest ingenuity was undoubtedly lavished on hairdos. One such capillary masterpiece, called *"au Parc Anglais,"* represented a model of the Regent's residence, the Palais-Royal, complete with gardens, basins, iron fences and coffeehouse. A very successful hairdo was the "sentimental pouf," which presented the touching picture of a mother surrounded by her baby, ots, and a little servant boy, the whole affair sprinkled with locks tak om the heads of her husband, father, father-in-law and other dear When Louis XV died, female heads mourned by covering themselv h artfully disposed miniature cypress trees. Women showed their ap tion of the blessings of science by adopting hairdos "*à l'Inoculatio.* hail the invention of the vaccination against smallpox; and they cele d the heroic feats of *La Belle Poule*, a brave little frigate which had fo . he English blockade during the American war for independence, by p it on their heads.

Nothing could stop the l —certainly not paternal admonitions. Witness the brief dialogue betw hilosopher Diderot and his daughter: He: "What have you got on head that makes it look as big as a pumpkin?" She: "It's an English ca " He: "But nobody can see you at the bottom of this so-called carr. She: "So much the better: people will look the more at me." Hai eached such dizzying heights that women had to kneel to get into th carriages—until Beaulard, one of those unjustly forgotten geniuses make life easier for the rest of mankind, invented a spring that d women to collapse their capillary monuments when passing throu ors. (These coiffures on springs were called "*à la grandmère*," beca rls would collapse them to avoid taunts of frivolity from Granny a them spring up again the minute the old folks were out of sight.)

The time-conscious Watteau was of course intensely preoccupied with fashion. The only original etchings he executed are a series of eight fashion plates *(page 78)*. His contemporaries had already noted this unusual interest. "His pictures," wrote a journalist less than a decade after Watteau's death, "may be regarded as the history of the fashions of his time." Doubly so, for Watteau, as has been said earlier, actually created some of them. He was the first major artist to concern himself with so minor a matter as fashion; but it is precisely a sign of his greatness that the light he threw on it no longer allows us to regard it as minor. Watteau taught us—if such a word may be applied to the least didactic of all artists—that fashions are the most graceful materialization of time.

We can only perceive time as passing, flowing, running. To defend ourselves against the dizziness which our awareness of it provokes in us, we try to concentrate on the present moment. The 18th Century developed a veritable cult of the moment. The chief pastime was love, for, as a celebrated ditty of the time puts it, "The pleasure of love lasts but an instant." Incisive and short-lived, witticisms—the favorite form of the age's *esprit*—had the sharpness (that is to say, the momentariness) of Cupid's arrows. Epicureanism—the philosophy of "enjoy life while ye may"—won more followers than any other. *No Tomorrow*, the title of a play of the period, aptly summarized the prevailing creed.

Art did not escape the general trend. "The painter has but a moment," declared Diderot. He meant that the artist could perceive and render only the briefest fraction of time. This was a sorry plight in an age that delighted in having paintings tell stories or develop actions, for action takes time to unfold. Eighteenth century artists solved this dilemma by representing, whenever possible, actions that could be contained in an in-

In Watteau's day the dress pictured above, like its shorter counterpart in the 1950s, was called a "sack." Because the artist dressed his painted females in it so often, however, it has also come to be known as the "Watteau gown." With voluminous sleeves and myriad pleats, its chief characteristic is the long, broad fold falling from the back of the neck to the ground.

stant: a lover hastily slipping a letter into a girl's hand while her mother is speaking to a servant; a young man kissing a lady's right hand while her old husband (who is presently asleep but who may wake up any moment) clutches her left hand; a beau hurriedly climbing into a closet while his companion frantically endeavors to repair the disorder of her clothes before her official protector enters her chamber. Passions are declared, love-pacts concluded, rendezvous arranged in less time than it takes to bat an eyelash, wave a fan or flash a smile.

Here again, Watteau paved the way, but as usual he displays a subtlety and a restraint unknown to his followers. The note which the figures in *The Concert* or *The Music Party* are holding is the present instant—a fraction of time so fleeting that extreme alertness and speed are needed to capture it. Watteau took great pains to acquire these qualities. His drawings multiply studies of people resting on one elbow, gripping the hilts of their swords, raising an arm or a foot. He made innumerable sketches of light briefly caressing a cheek, a neck, a satin fold—in short, quick motions and unstable equilibriums which possess only a momentary existence.

His friends marveled at his ability to catch a figure or a landscape in a few lightning strokes of the crayon. They also noted his habit of diluting his pigments in very fluid oils, so that his brush could move more rapidly about the canvas. At the latter practice they frowned, for it jeopardized the pictures' ability to last. Being dealers, like Sirois and Gersaint, or experts in the restoration and conservation of works of art, like Caylus, they warned Watteau against this danger. Yet he seemed not to care about his paintings' life expectancy and did not even bother to take the most elementary precautions. Caylus writes: "He took no care whatsoever of his colors; he barely replenished his palette every day and cleaned it even less; and his pot of fat oil, of which he made such great use, was filled with filth, dust and colors." It was as if Watteau felt that short-livedness was the price one had to pay for the art of capturing the fleeting moment.

And this is precisely the cruel truth which lends such a melancholy air, sometimes even a poignancy, to his *fêtes galantes*. Despite every effort, the beautiful note of the moment cannot be held indefinitely. The revelers are no more able to maintain themselves on the crest of the present than on the mound that swells up the ground they tread. With haunting frequency, figures turn their back to us and glide away, like mementos of the unavoidable hour of parting, of passing. Indeed, the sadness of parting is indivisible from the exquisitely enjoyable instant. Love, music, pleasures, beauty are so intense especially because they are so brief. Watteau's couples dance and glow like ephemerids in the deep transparency of twilight. By discovering time, Watteau had discovered that life was agonizingly vulnerable—in fact, that fragility was the sign of life. An almost imperceptible shiver runs through his personages, his trees, through the very texture of his painting—the shiver of life becoming conscious of its mortal nature.

No other artist ever succeeded in rendering that infinitesimal trembling. It is Watteau's supreme gift. Nowhere, perhaps, does it manifest itself more movingly than in his drawings. Black, red and white chalk stroke the paper as delicately as if it were a lady's cheek, but under the fine skin one senses the pulsing of life. Watteau's hand lingers on the most vulnerable, hence the most mobile parts, where the blood flows closest to the skin: a neck, a wrist, a temple, a quivering nostril. Silk, muslin, linen are animated by the same subliminal ripple, as if they were yet another kind of human skin. And after all, are they not made of the same fugitive substance? Is not life itself a beautiful moment, a short, graceful fashion? A hundred times, in the course of one drawing, Watteau makes light emerge from shadow and plunge into it again. The forms of life derive their extraordinary freshness from these incessant dawns, so closely tied to the intimation of coming darkness. One is reminded of a line in one of Voltaire's poems: "How close is morning to night!"

The verse from which the line comes deserves to be quoted at length, for it states clearly what the discovery of time meant at the level of every man's personal experience:

> *Tenderness, illusion, folly . . .*
> *How close is morning to night!*
> *I had but an hour, it is ended.*
> *We pass; the generation that follows ours*
> *Is already followed by another.*

"We are all like prisoners condemned to die," Voltaire wrote to his old friend, Mme. du Deffand: doubly condemned, for the intimation of mortality concerned society as well as the individual. The feverish indulgence in pleasures of every sort that characterizes the last phase of monarchic France is, quite simply, the prisoner's last meal. "Everything must end," Voltaire told Mme. du Deffand on another occasion. "Meanwhile, we must amuse ourselves." What makes Watteau different from the Lancrets and Paters who painted the same passing pleasures should now be clear: unlike his imitators, Watteau was agonizingly conscious of their impermanence, and he made this awareness an integral part of his work. That mysterious voice which, as we noted, makes his personages shiver and pause can be identified at last. When silence falls on a conversation, it is said that "an angel passes." The angel whose wings brush the gay participants in Watteau's parties, ever so lightly, causing them to hush, is the Angel of Death.

Although the mood of many of Watteau's pictures is one of tranquillity and happiness —couples exchanging loving glances, actors relaxing, children playing—this drawing of two skeletal angels carrying a weird garland of other skeletons reveals a sense of the macabre. Considering the artist's prolonged illness, it is not unlikely that he had—and perhaps pictured here— presentiments of an early death.

The Questin Line

Watteau was not only a sublime painter but also the finest draftsman of his era. He is even said to have preferred his drawings to his paintings, believing that he often could not render in oils the "spirit and truth which he knew how to give his crayon." And there is no question that Watteau's drawings speak eloquently, whether they are in the single color of red chalk called sanguine, or in the more elaborate three-color (red, white, black) technique that he had apparently learned from studying Rubens' drawings in Pierre Crozat's collection.

Watteau carried a notebook wherever he went, and sketched almost continuously, preferring to pick his subjects from life rather than hiring models to pose for him. The many volumes of sketches that he produced provided him with a rich supply of material for his paintings. His drawings seem to have served him as a kind of thesaurus from which he selected appropriate gestures or appealing attitudes, which he then wove almost spontaneously into his paintings. Thus, figures from the notebooks, like some of those shown on the following pages, appear again and again in Watteau's work. The kneeling male nude on page 90 was used in *Jupiter and Antiope (page 67)* and the young Negro appears in *The Music Party (page 72)*. But whether or not Watteau translated his sketches into fully modeled figures in oil, his sensitive and delicate line invariably captured the life, expression, grace and beauty of his subjects.

Grace, finesse, expression and, above all, economy characterize this masterful drawing. The merest strokes evoke the precise flare of a nostril, the exact set of the head upon the neck, the true fullness of a shoulder.

Woman seated

Bust of a woman, her head partly covered with a mantle

Reclining bacchante holding a g

Kneeling male nu

Seated man playing the guitar

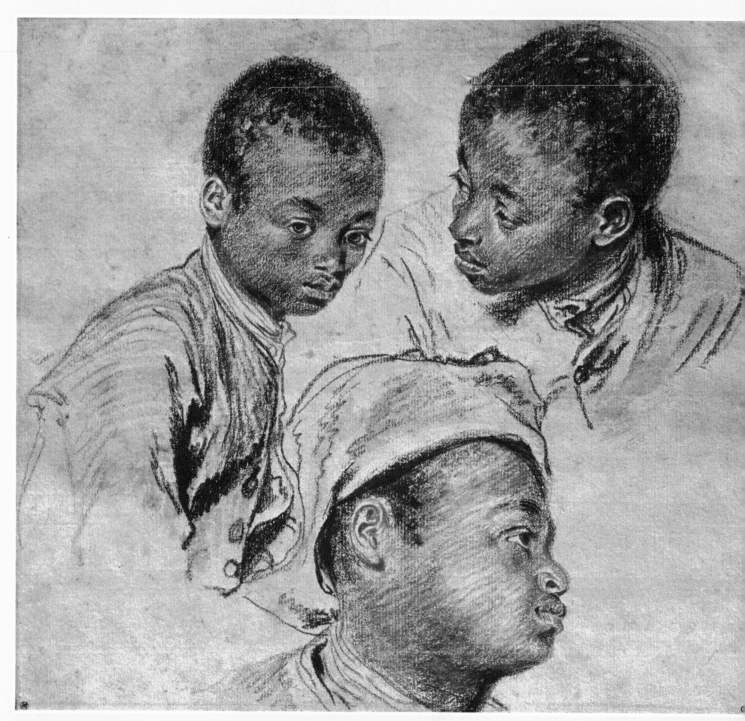

Three studies of a young Ne

Three studies of a woman, and a hand

Two studies of a young girl

Three studies of women and men

96

V

"Only His Palette Was Rosy"

...des are rare in Watteau's work, ...rhaps because on the eve of his ...ath he destroyed many of these ...uring pictures. This loss is a ...eat one, as this surviving ...inting shows; Watteau has ...ught a moment of perfect charm.

Lady at Her Toilet, 1719

Butterflies are not conscious of the shortness of time and the fragility of life. And, like all butterflies, the social butterflies during the age of the Regency and Louis XV were drawn hypnotically toward the fragrant flower of pleasure, and they fluttered from revel to carousal until they were sated. Nor do the aphorisms that were proclaimed—too loudly to be heartfelt—by writers like Voltaire bespeak a real familiarity with death; they belong in a large measure to the body of philosophic truisms handed down from antiquity. The unique shudder that runs through Watteau's work required a more intimate experience of mortality, for the sense of being vulnerable is something that must be felt day and night, in the flesh.

Such was the case with Watteau. Diderot's striking esthetic axiom, "The painter has only one moment at his disposal," can be applied to Watteau's life with chilling literalness. His health had been frail from childhood; probably this persuaded his parents to let him forsake the respectable family profession of roofmaker for the lowly one of painter. The years of misery had hardly improved the constitutional weakness of his lungs. By the time fame and prosperity came, tuberculosis had firmly struck root in his breast. For the last 10 years of his existence, Watteau carried his death within him.

His behavior seemed strange to his contemporaries and puzzled even his friends. They could not understand his restlessness. No sooner had he chosen a place of residence than he itched to leave it. Despite the pleasures and the security that he found at the mansion of Crozat, he soon departed. Sirois the dealer; Vleughels the Flemish painter and old-time friend; Jullienne the wealthy dye-manufacturer, supplier to the Gobelins, who had wanted to be a painter but, on Watteau's advice, became a superlatively discerning and generous patron of the arts—all sheltered him temporarily. Endlessly, he moved from address to address.

Restlessness, mobility, inconstancy of humor also governed Watteau's relations with his friends and his work. Frantic hope, feverish activity were invariably followed by disappointment, depression, apathy. He began his paintings enthusiastically but quickly grew disgusted with them.

It was as if he sought to conjure up on canvas the paradise that his life so little resembled, but soon realized that despite all his efforts the snake of time had insinuated itself into the Eden of the *fête galante*.

Long-term undertakings were unbearable to him; it took him five years and increasingly insistent reminders from the Academy to execute the reception piece required of every new member. According to his friend Gersaint, he preferred drawing to painting, no doubt because the former takes only a moment to complete—not long enough for the customary let-down to overtake him. Watteau's preference for small-size canvases may have been for the same reason. Large formats became more frequent only in his late years, when he had developed a brush technique of such swiftness and ease that he was able to finish a huge picture in less time than he once needed to complete a small one.

Often he treated his work with a negligence that bordered on contempt. Through the careless technique and the sloppiness that so upset his friends, collectors and dealers alike, he seemed to say: "These paintings do not deserve to survive." And indeed he would often wipe them out. People regarded his attitude as a mixture of modesty and foolishness. In exchange for a wig he gave a wigmaker two of his precious little oils and reproached himself with not having given the man a third to make the barter less unfair.

Worried about Watteau's indifference to his own fate, Caylus one day read him a severe lecture. In the grimmest terms, he described the future of misery, hunger and illness awaiting the painter if he did not act more carefully. Watteau listened to the Count's good sense and replied quietly: "If worse comes to worst, there is always the public hospital. They don't turn away anybody there, do they?"

How strange Watteau's modesty seems by the standards of his age! He disliked money; he did not think he himself deserved it; moreover it was, in his eyes, the proof that he was practicing a trade. While other artists of his epoch and previous ones had accepted—and even welcomed—this condition, Watteau was irritated by it. He did not view art as a trade but as a goal in itself. To his contemporaries, art was still a way to earn a living; to him, it was an instrument for a kind of personal salvation. Watteau did not consider that his painting was incompetent; he merely looked upon it with disdain—or rather with the rancor that comes of great expectations unfulfilled, for it did not bring him the spiritual release he so desperately desired.

Watteau was the first major French painter since Le Brun; yet they seem to belong to different planets. Le Brun could work well only amidst the turmoil and the slavery brought by servile flatterers and tyrannical patrons; Watteau preferred obscurity to glory, because it guaranteed his liberty. Not once did he try to obtain a royal commission, nor did the Regent, that indefatigable collector, purchase a single one of his paintings. The Academy would have brought him that asset so valuable in society, "connections"; Watteau attended its weekly meetings only twice. He, who left us so many evocations of graceful social life, fled the world. Secrecy was second nature to him. Few painters have so successfully foiled the curiosity of scholars; though he lived only 250 years ago and in an age where one's slightest move immediately became the talk of the town, his biography is hardly better known than that of Giotto, who lived in the 14th Century.

Not even his close friends escaped the manifestations of his misanthropy. He could be delightful company, for he was generous and devoted to those he loved. He was witty, a sharp observer of mankind, and by dint of intelligence and thoughtful reading he had compensated for the scantiness of his early education. But of a sudden, the horrible companion within his body would raise its voice, audible to him alone; then he would lapse into gloom or show signs of impatience, or irritation, and depart. Or else, more bewilderingly still, he would become strangely absent amidst the most amicable and animated gathering, exactly like the *commedia dell'arte* character Gilles that he so often depicted. Gilles, white as candor, exploited by everyone, yet indifferent, eyes vacant, arms dangling, a distracted smile on his lips, silent amidst talk and action, a melancholy dreamer among gay doers, solitary in the thick of society—certainly Watteau identified himself unconsciously with this character. Again and again we meet this figure in the painter's work, as if the burden of his secret weighed so heavily on Watteau that he could not refrain from presenting us a lucid if coded confession. His contemporaries often wondered how the creator of so many joyous scenes could be so brooding. Watteau's imaginary self-portraits give the answer: Gilles' melancholia is necessary to make people laugh. Clowns (Pagliaccio is a first cousin to Gilles) are sad. As the 19th Century poet and critic Théophile Gautier rightly said about Watteau: "Only his palette was rosy."

Gilles only appears indifferent to the scenes of love-making and merry-making that surround him. They are a dream he is dreaming; awaken him and the magic fades at once. Watteau daydreamed the pleasures that his faltering physical condition prevented him from tasting in reality. The artist who, more than any other, deserves to be called the painter of love seems to have had practically no relations with women. He did not marry, and if he had a mistress he kept her successfully hidden. Not once throughout his existence is a woman's name, a woman's presence, associated with him. The lusty Caylus was probably right when he said: "All his love-making was mental."

In every way Watteau, like the Gilles of his pictures, remains remote. In a world where the essential acts of life were carried out in the presence of outsiders, where women gave birth, spouses entered their nuptial beds, and men died before a more or less interested crowd of neighbors and acquaintances, Watteau was inventing something unknown till then: the sense of privacy. The poetic distance at which his *fêtes galantes* seem to take place in his paintings is the exact measure of the distance that he preserved between himself and other people, especially those who threatened to come closest to him: the friends he loved.

He kept his secret well. Nothing transpired from his looks. "He had no physiognomy whatsoever," noted Caylus. His rare portraits, by himself or by others, all show the same absent, distant, enigmatic face. There is an undefinable air of diffidence about it, an almost deliberate inexpressiveness. It is broad and ungainly. The eyes are deepset, neutral;

Watteau's drawing of the *commedia dell'arte* figure Gilles captures the lonely sadness of that fellow, perpetually beset by his master's demands, his own laziness and his friends' misunderstandings. The character had been established by 1673, when French writers collaborating with the Italian players of *commedia dell'arte* wrote Gilles into many plots where he served as a foil. Watteau, an outsider in his society, must have been emotionally attracted to the character.

the sensuous mouth is twisted at its extremities by two bitter wrinkles; the nose, long and bony, is fastidiously drawn up, as if smelling some unpleasant odor; long-fingered, emaciated hands emerge from lace-lined sleeves. If one did not know Watteau's age, one would never have guesssed that the model of these portraits was a young man.

But was he? In 1717, when he completed *Pilgrimage,* he was 33 years old. Four years later he would be dead. Comparing a man's life to the sun's trajectory from dawn to dusk, one might say that Watteau's course was not cut off abruptly at noon, but accelerated, so that he reached evening more quickly than is customary. He died worn out, old at 37. Much of this acceleration occurred during those last four years; into them are compressed 40 years of a normal existence.

The development of his work mirrors this speed-up. Watteau's art evolved more swiftly in a few months than the work of others might in a decade. Nothing illustrates this change more dramatically than *Pilgrimage.* For there exists a second version of it; its exact date is uncertain, but it was painted before 1719—less than two years after the first version. The two pictures *(pages 106-107 and 108-109)* are worlds apart; and the fact that the later version was meant as a simple copy of the earlier brings out still more plainly the difference between them.

Both are concerned with the same Cytherean scene, but version Number One depicts it, so to speak, at sunrise, whereas version Number Two presents it at noon. In Number One, figures and landscape are wrapped in a subtle, pervasive haze that confers on all things a trembling, dimly lit indecision. Reality seems dream, dream seems reality in the poetic mist.

In Number Two, the midday sun has dissipated the haze. The mountains have evaporated into the blue. The vague, quivering bowers have thickened into real vegetation: you can now count the trees and tell their species. Hint has given way to statement, evocation to affirmation. The deep golden overall harmony has exploded into a dozen bright patches of color. These lovely silk dresses are no longer the work of fairies' hands, but of the dressmakers on Rue Saint-Honoré; and there is nothing ethereal about the lovers who wear them. Adolescent, morning love is content with reverie: mature love wants more material sustenance.

The most striking illustration of Watteau's evolution is provided by the two new couples introduced on the right side of Number Two. The pair in front are engaged in an activity to which the artist had not accustomed us: they are embracing. The two behind them are gathering flowers, a pastime whose pertinence we shall easily understand if we remember that the English expression "to flirt" is the phonetic transcription of the Old French *"fleureter,"* meaning literally "to talk flowers."

The changes noticeable in the second version of *Pilgrimage* are evident in all the work produced between 1717 and 1719. The themes remain the same, but their presentation is more sensual, more material; sunlight has dried up the vapors of nostalgia. The poetic distance has been narrowed, and what seemed imaginary now looks real.

The hands: one need only look at those painted and drawn by Watteau in these years of growing illness to understand how little he was made for gorging and glutting. Once one's attention has been caught by them, one can see nothing else in the paintings; they become an obsession—as indeed they did for Watteau, who drew scores of them in his sketchbooks during this period. One finds bony, hungry, pleading hands, strained and flushed by the effort to grasp, to clasp, like a bird's claws on the branch shaken by a storm. They hold on to the lady's waist, the guitar, the sword's grip for dear life. Every one of these frail hands proclaims Watteau's panic at feeling life inexorably slipping away from him.

He was reaching that point of anxiety and despair when people suffering from incurable diseases lend their ear to the promises of quacks. In 1719 Watteau suddenly decided to go to England, where there lived a charlatan who claimed that no case of consumption could resist his skill. Rumors of quick and easy money for artists from the continent may also have contributed to his decision, for the avid, grasping quality revealed by the hands he drew and painted seems also to have affected the ailing artist's character. He stopped giving his things away. He now craved wealth as well as health, and fancied that to find them he needed only to cross the Channel. Vainly his friends sought to dissuade him.

He arrived in London unknown and practically unintroduced. Quite naturally, he joined the colony of French artists who had set up their headquarters at Old Slaughter's Tavern on St. Martin's Lane, in the heart of London's theater district. Here these voluntary exiles met to stave off homesickness and exchange information about potential patrons. These were quite numerous, for English painting had not yet reached an international level of competence and there were plenty of opportunities for continental artists. Watteau, who towered above his colleagues in London, easily found outlets for his work. Gainsborough and the polite English school of the second half of the century owe much to the canvases he painted for English connoisseurs.

Watteau's health, however, was quite another story. The promised miracle cure of course proved to be bogus and the rigors of the British climate only aggravated Watteau's condition. When he returned to Paris, in 1720, his health was irretrievably wrecked. So was his wealth, some of which he had invested in John Law's Company of the Indies. The Scotsman's castles in Spain—or rather in America—were beginning to collapse. Daily, the crowds of panic-stricken investors grew larger and more menacing, till at last Law was spirited out of the country. Thousands had been ruined by the world's first full-fledged stockmarket crash; among them were many artists, including Watteau's erstwhile master Gillot. Watteau himself made a humorous allusion to the event in a semi-mythological drawing that shows a party of disheveled survivors reaching the shore, where they are greeted by people in modern dress, while Neptune, his Tritons and his horses, are hot on their trail. Someone had indeed rescued Watteau from his financial shipwreck—at least partially: his patron and friend, the dyemaker Jullienne, who salvaged some 6,000 livres of his savings before it was too late. However, these monetary setbacks were overshadowed by the impending loss of a far more precious possession: life itself.

Too feeble to live alone, Watteau accepted Gersaint's hospitality. Gersaint occupied a house on the Pont Notre-Dame. His gallery, "The

Because of its flexibility and mobility, the human hand is extremely difficult to draw. Watteau, who made these six studies of the left hand of an actor gesturing, at rest and toying with a box, captured the expressiveness and individuality of the hand with a mastery achieved by few artists.

Great Monarch," was on the ground floor and he lived upstairs with his family. Watteau was thus back on the bridge that had been the scene of his miserable, clumsy beginnings. And there a miracle occurred—an artistic, not a medical miracle. Watteau painted a sign for Gersaint's shop —"to limber up his fingers," the art dealer said. The 64-inch by 121-inch sign took Watteau only eight days to paint. "And," adds Gersaint, "he worked on it only in the morning, at that," for he was terribly weakened by illness. Perhaps it was this breathtaking speed that caused Watteau to consider *Gersaint's Shop Sign (pages 110-111)* the one truly acceptable picture he ever painted: he had not time to grow dissatisfied with it. As for Gersaint, he would have preferred his friend to save his ebbing strength for more "serious" work. But when he hung the huge sign in the arcade, under the weatherboard outside his shop, crowds were drawn to it as if by magic. Within a few weeks, the picture, one of the greatest in Western art, was purchased by a Parisian collector, thereby escaping the usual fate of shop signs.

The spell still works; magic is not too strong a word. This picture about art is so lifelike as to make one forget that it is a work of art. It shows the inside of Gersaint's gallery exactly as the passerby could see it. In the foreground is the street; the walls are lined with canvases for sale, and these pictures within the picture, as well as the glittering mirrors and windowpanes in the back lend, by contrast, still more reality to the actors of the scene: Gersaint and his helpers showing paintings and knicknacks to clients; a connoisseur helping a lady up the step; two employees crating the portrait of Louis XIV while a lackey stands by; a flea-pestered dog curled on the cobblestones.

A picture of life? Rather, life itself. A moment of human time, not arrested, but happening forever. Delicacy, polished manners, elegance, refined taste—the quintessence of that fragile product which is called civilization has been caught in the peak of its flower by the fragile painter most capable of rendering it.

What has made the miracle of *Gersaint's Shop Sign* possible? First, of course, is the absolute mastery attained at this stage by Watteau. If we free ourselves from the spell cast by the huge picture and step closer till illusion is no longer possible, we discover another wonder: the fabulous freedom, deftness and assurance of his brush. In his youth, he could do only one thing: compact figures, contained by a continuous outline. In his mature phase he replaced that heavy, continuous outline with running, breaking, nervous strokes and with scintillating highlights playing on them. In his final manner, light, color and form are inseparable. There are no more asperities, no more breaks. The nuances, the halftones are richer than ever before, the brushstrokes so broad, so loose and casual as to seem almost random, yet woven into one single fabric, blended into indivisible unity.

The freedom, the unity—they lead us to the heart of the miracle. Between the magic of lifelikeness of the *Shop Sign* seen at a distance and the magic of paint revealed at close range, there seems to be no connection. That extraordinary, whiplike white-and-blue stroke, for instance, does not imitate the embroidery on the coat of the man on the far right:

After Watteau painted his famous shop sign for the art dealer Gersaint *(pages 110-111)*, François Boucher made this business card for the dealer, who then sold everything from sea shells to Oriental bric-a-brac, in addition to paintings and jewelry. To meet the vogue for *chinoiserie*, Gersaint had changed the character of his merchandise and the name of his shop, called "The Pagoda."

it *is* embroidery. Realism self-consciously seeks to render reality. *Gersaint's Shop Sign* is reality.

Had we any doubt about the forces at work in *Gersaint's Shop Sign*, we need only turn to a painting that may have been executed very soon after it, *Gilles (page 113)*. Watteau always spoke most personally through the figure of Gilles. But here, in the last of the series, is the artist's testament. Better, it is the sweeping, dispassionate glance cast on his life by someone who is already on the way to another shore. The picture is eerily serene, disquieting through the otherworldliness with which it treats the world. The latter, in all its frivolity, is at Gilles' feet—in fact, *on* his feet, in the shape of two huge, ridiculous pink ribbons adorning his slippers. Intrigue, lust, mockery, symbolized by *commedia dell'arte* characters, swarm about him. Gilles' fate is to be victimized. He knows it, accepts it—silent, meek and long-suffering as the donkey behind him. His hands no longer seek to grasp, to hold on; they hang limply. And because of the completeness of his acceptance an extraordinary transfiguration now takes place. The figure of Gilles becomes more and more monumental, outgrows the agitation at its feet, soars heavenward. Watteau, the painter of other people's passions, here represents his own life and career as a re-enactment of the Passion.

Watteau did not stay long with Gersaint. Anxiety soon caught up with him and he moved to other quarters, and others still, driven by a frenzy that we recognize only too well as symptomatic of the end. Early in 1721 he expressed the wish to settle outside of Paris because he felt that the fresh air would do him good. His ever-solicitous friends placed at his disposal a house at Nogent on the Marne.

There Watteau prepared for death. Although his work was untinged by obscenity, he tried to recuperate in order to destroy—fortunately for us, he only partly succeeded—the few nudes he had painted. More and more, his mind turned to religion. For his parish priest at Nogent he painted a picture of Christ on the Cross. Whenever he felt strong enough he took up his pencil or his brush. Even atonement assumed artistic form. Some years earlier Watteau had taken a novice painter from Valenciennes, Jean-Baptiste Pater, under his protection. Soon, however, the irritable master could no longer bear the continual presence of his student, and gave him his leave. Repenting his rudeness, Watteau called Pater back and, for the last weeks of his life, made him work under his guidance and painted in his presence. Later, Pater declared that he had learned all he knew about art in those precious days.

They were few. A dying man's thoughts turn to the time of his beginnings, and Watteau planned to return to his hometown, Valenciennes. But he was not to nurture this vain hope very long. He was by now too weak to get out of bed. It is reported that, as he lay there, the priest of Nogent presented him a crucifix for him to kiss. Watteau found it badly carved and said: "Take away this crucifix, it makes me feel sorry. Is it possible that my Master should have been so badly treated?"

He died on July 18, 1721. Crozat wrote to a painter friend: "We have lost poor Watteau, who finished his days, brush in hand." Like Raphael and Van Gogh, Antoine Watteau died at the age of 37.

Boucher honored Watteau in this allegory: the toppled easel refers to his early death; the canvas depicts a detail from *A Pilgrimage to Cythera*. The inscription reads, "The Graces, who in Watteau's incomparable works offer the eye their smiling likeness everywhere, now shed their tears upon his tomb."

The Masterpieces

Watteau's greatest paintings were made during the last five years of his life. They were years when illness and bad fortune robbed him of his remaining strength and security and when, although his friends clustered around him, he shrugged off all comfort and isolated himself. Yet in this tortured period he reached the peak of his abilities. His brush had acquired a dazzling skill and speed—one of those late paintings was made in just over a week, and at that, the painter had only worked mornings. But more than technical dexterity, Watteau had achieved the full power of an artist's vision; he transformed the *fête galante* into a poem of love in two versions of *A Pilgrimage to Cythera;* he elevated the sad clown of the *commedia dell'arte* into a tragic hero; and he wrote the epitaph for an age in a huge painting made to serve as a signboard for an art dealer.

Devoted to the end to the magic of the theater, Watteau especially enjoyed the improvisatory wit of the *commedia dell'arte.* Fittingly, the characters that he apparently loved best and pictured most often were two who seem to resemble him, Gilles and Mezzetino. Like Watteau, who felt himself an outsider in society, these characters are outsiders in their play situations; Gilles is a clown pushed about by others yet able to see others' foibles clearly, and Mezzetino *(right)* is a valet with a quick wit and a sharp tongue. Through them, he delivered his last and most poignant message.

Mezzetino, called Mezzetin in France, changed character with the actor who played him. It was not an actor, however, but a friend whom Watteau chose to wear the most typical Mezzetino costume for this small painting.

Mezzetin, c. 1719

On August 28, 1717, Watteau presented his painting *A Pilgrimage to Cythera* to the Academy and was finally received as a full member. He had been an associate for five years but so little did he care about the honors and career opportunities that Academy membership could offer him that he postponed preparing his reception piece. Finally, at the urging of the Academicians he delivered this magnificent picture.

It is a picture of love, and every element speaks of the theme. The place to which the pilgrims have come is the fabled island where Venus rose from the sea; at the extreme right is a bust of Venus, the Goddess of Love, and it is adorned with roses and twined vines, perhaps symbolic of lovers' embracings. On the pedestal of the statue hang a bow and arrows, Cupid's darts. Indeed, Cupid is everywhere; the amorous *putti* of Italian mythological paintings fly about urging the lovers on.

But Watteau's couples are restrained; they engage in hushed conversation, move quietly about. These pilgrims—their staffs and traveling costumes identify them as such—seem reluctant to leave their dreamy idyll and return to land, to reality.

Thus, long understood as a departure *for* the island of love—because of a mistitled engraving—the picture is now seen as a departure *from* Cythera. The wistful mood, the golden tones, the gentle interchanges between these courtly ladies and gentlemen, chatting under Venus' gaze, make Watteau's purpose clear.

A Pilgrimage to Cythera, 1717

For unknown reasons Watteau painted a second version of his *Pilgrimage,* probably no more than two years after the first. It seems to have been intended as a simple copy of the earlier painting, perhaps for a collector-friend, but the result turned out to be dramatically different.

Here, the mists of reverie have blown away and the pilgrims are revealed in full light. Everything has become more explicit, more substantial; even the putti *(above)* are fleshier, more active. The statue bust of Venus has become a full-length, almost live woman; the boat has become a real ship and not a vaporous illusion. Finally, Watteau has included a new pair of lovers who, unlike the couples in the first version, are in a full embrace and are being garlanded with roses by three cupids.

What can account for this transformation? Did Watteau sense his nearing death—and seek to fight it with a portrayal of a more solid, earthier love? Had his illness stripped him of the power to fantasize? No one will ever know, of course, but these two brilliant pictures provoke fascinating questions about the workings of an artist's mind.

A Pilgrimage to Cythera, between 1717 and 1719

109

One of the greatest pictures Watteau ever painted was made for his friend Gersaint. This painting was done in eight days, an extremely short period for any painting, and phenomenal for a work as accomplished as this one. Indeed, its freshness and vibrant color are at least partly a result of Watteau's speed. Its subject is simple—the

salesroom of Gersaint's shop as it is seen from the street —but a subtle theme is interwoven. In the left-hand corner a portrait of the late King Louis XIV is being packed away perhaps suggesting the end of an era. But as always, Watteau is never mawkish about such passings. It is a statement of fact, made candidly and without regret.

Gersaint's Shop Sign, 1720

111

Watteau's genius is perhaps most poignantly revealed in two late paintings of the *commedia dell'arte* character Gilles—a figure in whom Watteau invested many of his most personal feelings. Both of these works were painted within the last two years of Watteau's life, at a time when he undoubtedly knew that the terrible destroyer within his chest—tuberculosis—would kill him.

If *Gilles* is not the very last painting he made it can surely stand for it. Like *Gersaint's Shop Sign, Gilles* was probably painted as a signboard—for a Paris theater, on whose stage the painter had undoubtedly enjoyed the antics of the clowns. And in this work the final isolation of the artist-clown is most strongly pictured. Gilles has become a monumental figure, larger than life. Though he is surrounded by the world's vices—the other characters in the painting represent lust, intrigue and mockery—he is alone. His hands hang limply down, unable even to reach out for the last comforts of the world; the play is over.

Gilles, c. 1721

VI

The Reign of a Royal Favorite

Prophetically, the central figure Watteau had painted in his masterpiece, *Gersaint's Shop Sign*, is a woman. In the period that begins with his death, art became feminine business. Soon, a woman would exert on the epoch an influence as powerful as that of Colbert and his collaborators during the previous reign—so powerful, in fact, that she has become identified with its tastes, its art, its style. The age of Louis XIV could be known by no other name; the age of Louis XV is at least as familiar under that of a lady born the very year Watteau died.

The name by which she was known for much of her life was Jeanne-Antoinette Poisson. Poisson in French means "fish," and the name was eminently suitable. M. Poisson, a merchant, belonged to the small fry that swam in the wake of the great sharks of aristocracy. After a business scandal he went abroad, leaving his wife in Paris; and Jeanne-Antoinette was born during that peri... A financier called Le Normant de Tournehem, a good friend of Mme. Poisson—she was the kind of woman whose friends tend to be financiers—took a paternal interest in the child.

It was he who supervised her education. And quite an education it was. The best ballet masters and musicians taught her to sing and dance; France's most famous tragic playwright, Prosper Jolyot Crébillon, gave her lessons in diction. She became an accomplished horsewoman and a frequenter of the salons of Mme. Geoffrin and Mme. de Tencin, where the conversation of the most distinguished writers, artists and thinkers of the day whetted her wits and sharpened her tongue.

When she was 20, Le Normant de Tournehem married her to his nephew, Charles-Guillaume Le Normant. Although the marriage elevated her social status and improved her financial position, it was merely one further step in young Jeanne's ascent; it enabled her to gather around her, in her country house of Etioles, a select band of courtly libertines, like Voltaire and the future Cardinal de Bernis, who refused to celebrate Mass with anything but vintage wines in order not to wince in the face of the Lord. To them the coolheaded young woman and her designing mother disclosed their extraordinary ambition: Jeanne was to be to Louis XV what Mme. de Maintenon had been to Louis XIV.

A gypsy, so the story goes, had predicted to her, when she was a child, that she would be the King's mistress, and she had prepared herself for that calling ever since. Following the prophecy her mother nicknamed Jeanne-Antoinette "Reinette"—little queen. It seemed a far-fetched hope. The young monarch with the pretty girl's face had at first seemed interested only in hunting. Next, married to the pious, graceless Princess Marie Leczinska of Poland, he had behaved as a very dutiful husband. Ten children were born of their union, of whom seven survived, six girls and one boy. Six to one: it was like a statistical confirmation of the dominant part played by women throughout the century. Indeed, one man now chose to pretend he was a woman in order to get ahead. This was the Chevalier d'Eon, who lived most of his life as a transvestite. Legend has it that he succeeded in getting himself hired as a lady in attendance to Empress Elizabeth of Russia, and despite this, was later sent to London where he served as the King's Minister Plenipotentiary.

Louis XV was long in falling prey to women, but when he did he made up for lost time. This did not increase young Mme. d'Etioles' chances notably, for the King seemed bent upon selecting his mistresses from a particular family—the de Nesles. One sister followed another in the royal favors—and there were at least three and possibly four of them. But in 1744, the last of them died, and Jeanne-Antoinette decided that her time had come. In 1745, a costume ball took place at Versailles, with the King and several other participants disguised as trees. Jeanne-Antoinette was there in the dress of Diana, the huntress, and she so

teased and tantalized Louis XV that he asked her to take off her mask. That was the beginning. Later, she was temporarily installed in one of the King's private apartments. Having achieved her ambition, she left her husband; a deed of separation was later conveniently granted by the Parisian parliament. In September 1745, a few months after meeting the King, Jeanne-Antoinette was formally presented to the court under the hastily bestowed title of Marquise de Pompadour.

This kind of relationship should logically have lasted a few weeks; Louis XV was fickle and sensual, the Marquise de Pompadour was ravishing but frigid. It lasted nearly 20 years, until she died: 20 years during which she was the uncrowned Queen of France—she ended by saying "We" instead of "I" and having visitors stand in her presence—despite continuous, ruthless intriguing to topple her from her powerful and widely envied position.

How she did it must stand as a tribute to her intelligence and charm, if not to her morals. Louis XV suffered from a most uncomfortable disease: deep, incurable ennui. Pompadour realized that the best way to hold him was to entertain him better than anybody else. She became his minister of pleasures. When she could no longer assuage the King's sexual appetites, she reconciled herself to his pursuit of such pleasures elsewhere. But she remained his best friend and closest confidante. (Indeed, Pompadour was so gracious and eager to please that she even won the affections of the Queen.) Her apartments became a haven of distractions where the King could escape the rigid etiquette of the court. There,

The King and several noblemen came disguised as yew trees when a masked ball was held at Versailles in 1745. That night he met the witty and fascinating young woman who, within a few short months, became the Marquise de Pompadour. His mistress for 20 years, she wielded considerable power behind the throne of France and was a generous supporter of artists and writers.

she had a private theater built. Her friends—Voltaire, among others—wrote the plays, which were performed by the Marquise and by people of the court. Pompadour thus leveled a running fire of amusements at Louis XV's boredom. She strove to make his private life a perpetual celebration. To provide its continually renewed setting she needed a superlative stage designer, a master decorator. She found him in the person of François Boucher.

Boucher was born on September 29, 1703, the son of a mediocre painter and of a woman of modest origins. When the young François showed an inclination to follow his father's profession, he was apprenticed, in about 1720, to François Le Moine, who was regarded by contemporaries as the major artist of the time, the painter most qualified to uphold the tradition of heroic decoration established by Le Brun. Times had changed, however, and the epic mood was becoming increasingly difficult to sustain. Le Moine himself was to illustrate this tragically. For three years he worked on his *magnum opus*, the ceiling of the Salon d'Hercule, at Versailles. But the grandiose proportions and intentions of the *Apotheosis of Hercules* proved too much of a strain on him. His mind became unhinged and, in 1737, scarcely a year after the triumphal unveiling of his ceiling, Le Moine, in a fit of madness, stabbed himself to death with his sword.

His disciple Boucher ran no such risk. He was not the man to strain. Le Moine had sought to reconcile the Classic ideal with Rococo taste by lending it lightness and brilliancy. Boucher adapted Le Moine's tactics to his own use. He took over the brilliance and rejected the heroics. With Boucher, the gods step down from Olympus into boudoirs. The same six-to-one ratio that occurred among Louis XV's progeny applies to the cast of Boucher's paintings. Women, alluringly undressed, are everywhere; Venus, surrounded by her retinue of cupids, triumphs. Male figures are few and uninteresting, and their actions revolve entirely around the gentler sex. Thus, *The Rising of the Sun* shows Apollo leaving Thetis' bed and the companion picture, *The Setting of the Sun,* shows him returning to it.

Gods, however, even when they revel, will be gods; an air of solemnity lingers about them despite their roguish demeanor. Boucher needed more casual, modern subject matter to add zest to his work. He was soon to find it. He had left Le Moine's studio after a short time, and, in 1721, entered that of the engraver Jean-François Cars. There he not only learned the techniques of engraving but was able to give vent for the first time to his fabulous facility. With untiring energy he provided designs and illustrations for books, brochures, leaflets, diplomas, and so on. His skill came to the attention of Jean de Jullienne who, as a tribute to his friend Watteau, had decided to have the latter's works engraved. It was a huge and costly undertaking, requiring the services of a whole team of printmakers. In 1725, Boucher joined their ranks; he was quickly to prove the best of them.

Watteau's pictures, which Boucher could now contemplate at will in Jullienne's collection, provided the young painter with the worldly dimension he had not found in Le Moine. He was quick to recognize that, in the reign of the youthful Louis XV, this was the way to dress and to act on Cythera. He took over the flirtatious shepherds and shepherdesses, the bantering peasants, the idyllic landscapes, the festive spirit, the games, the elegance, the social atmosphere, the sprightly, witty manner. But he did not assimilate Watteau's secret melancholia and masked profundity. Boucher is all surface and no mystery.

Boucher was unlike Watteau in another respect as well: he neither was nor wished to be an outsider. He was not content to dream about the good things of life, and he knew that to obtain them he needed a successful career, the road to which inevitably led through the Academy. In 1724, therefore, he entered its yearly competition for painters. The imposed subject was undoubtedly one of the most soporific ever proposed: "Evilmerodach, son and successor of Nebuchadnezzar, delivering Joachim from the chains in which his father had kept him fettered for so long." Remote as this theme was from Boucher's inclinations, his dexterity was such that he won first prize.

Three years later, having earned enough money by working as an engraver, he took the next step in a proper career—a sojourn in Rome. The Eternal City had little to offer 18th Century artists like Boucher except the prestige of a glorious past. He spent the years from 1727 to 1731 at the French Academy in Rome, then directed by Watteau's friend Nicolas Vleughels. For a painter who boasted, much later in life, that he took the trip "for curiosity's rather than utility's sake" and who found Raphael "trite," the Carracci "murky" and Michelangelo "hunchbacked," four years is a long time—unless the objects of his curiosity were the beautiful young damsels rather than the masterpieces of Italy.

Indeed, he seems to have interpreted in a distinctly personal way the classical axiom: follow nature. "Boucher was young, handsome; he loved beautiful women as well as beautiful pictures," reports a contemporary chronicle, "and never did a pretty model leave his studio before she had granted him her last favors." The latter could not have been exceedingly difficult to obtain, for he chose his models at the Opéra, which seemed to be in the process of becoming a national brothel. Despite the fact that its members received no wages, the Opéra's *corps de ballet* mustered four times as many women as it needed, because any girl eager to trade on her charms was sure to find a wealthy protector there—as well as sanctuary from the vexations exerted by the authorities on less artistic forms of prostitution.

The ladies of Boucher's pictures cannot altogether disguise their real occupation. A trace of vulgarity lurks underneath their elegance. The nymphs and divinities are opera-girls in disguise. On stage—that is, on canvas—they behave properly enough, but there is something about their gaze and their attitudes that leads one to think that they will quickly pass to more relaxed pastimes the moment the curtain falls. Decency, in Boucher's painting, is often but a spice, a transparent veil easily torn by the spectator's imagination. "Boucher had not seen the graces in the right sort of places," his contemporary Jean-François Marmontel wrote.

Boucher's own wife was extremely pretty, and only 17 when he married her in 1733. He was already a man of 30. When he asked his friend, Louis Petit de Bachaumont, what he should read to find themes for a series of canvases on the story of Psyche, the writer sent him a reading list and added: "But above all, look carefully at Mme. Boucher." He did, and she often posed for him *(pages 130, 132-133)*. She also attracted others. The great Swedish collector, Count Tessin, wrote an insipid little fairy tale that he asked Boucher to illustrate as a pretext to see the artist's wife more often. This was not difficult, for Mme. Boucher had learned to paint miniatures and to engrave, and was now working in her husband's studio. Even in her old age, she remained coquettish and continued to follow the fashion. It annoyed her that in the portrait Latour had painted of her when she was young, she should be shown wearing a hairdo that had gone out of style; she therefore asked the neoclassicist Jacques-Louis David to update it.

In his work, as in his life, Boucher was thus committed to love. "He had stolen Venus' belt," as a critic of the time put it. But how different was his kind of love from the exquisite delicacy of Watteau! Sensuality had taken the place of sentiment, the amorous had given way to the erotic. "This fellow takes up his brush only to show breasts and buttocks," exclaimed the critic Denis Diderot in exasperation.

It is this very shift that accounts for Boucher's popularity. For the age of Louis XV subscribed wholeheartedly to Chamfort's famous epigram: "Love is the contact between two skins." Boucher's glorification of skin-deep love was bound to delight an epoch that had taken to its heart Bernis' motto: "For the present moment, always a pleasure; for the coming hour, always a desire"; an epoch that regarded physical love as the strongest antidote for the boredom that besets any idle society. Immorality—in fact, amorality—became the rule. "Virtue," said one distinguished woman, "is nothing more today than the name for a kind of ribbon you fasten with pins." Scientists like Georges de Buffon, one of the fathers of the modern natural sciences, shared this view: "The only good part of love is the physical." Boucher's acid critic Diderot shared it, too—that is, as long as age allowed him to. Recalling his youth, he summed it up by a formula that also fits Boucher's art to perfection: "Women, very little mystery, no sincerity!"

The reign of Louis XV was the golden age of vice not because its immorality was greater than that of other periods but because it had more allure. It practiced its vices so elegantly that they could be mistaken for virtues. Such was its virtuosity at preserving appearances that we almost forget—and they certainly did—that there was anything to be ashamed of. No one possessed this allure, this elegance, this virtuosity more than Boucher. He was unequaled in the art of redeeming petty instincts by treating them in the grand manner. Boucher's work does not have style, but it is stylish.

Naughty, stylish, decorative: this was the man the Marquise de Pompadour needed. But he was not exactly her discovery. Boucher's prestige was already well established when she became the King's favorite. He had been received into the Academy in 1734, had executed several royal commissions and had won the enthusiastic support of many patrons. The artist whom Pompadour enlisted was in the full flower of his maturity—

Of all the artists to win the support of the Marquise de Pompadour, François Boucher was the most favored. He designed this actor's costume for a theatrical troupe and dressed the sets for many of the private entertainments Pompadour put on to amuse the King. Boucher's works so pleased Louis XV that he became First Painter to the King, even though by the time he received this honor Pompadour was dead.

and had to be, for she wanted him not only to distract the jaded Louis XV but also to set the tone for the whole kingdom. She had chosen him, in a word, to be her Le Brun.

Surprising as it may seem, for conquerors of women are not usually slaves of work, Boucher lived up to her expectations. If he dissipated all night, he painted all day, every day of his existence. His creative energy was immense; he once claimed that he had done more than a thousand paintings, and 10,000 drawings in his life. The pictures ordered by Pompadour for her various manors, and by every self-respecting member of society who felt that he simply must own a work by the fashionable artist, would have been enough to exhaust an ordinary man. Yet Boucher shouldered many more tasks. He designed sets and costumes for the Opéra, the Opéra-Comique and the Théâtre de la Foire. He provided cartoons for the tapestries woven at the Royal Beauvais factory, as well as for the Gobelins, of which he became the Inspector. He furnished motifs and models for one of Pompadour's pet projects, the Royal Porcelain Manufacture of Sèvres, whose products rivaled and eventually eclipsed those produced by other European centers. From his pencil flowed an endless stream of visual ideas for fountains, garden statuary, prints, vases, jewels, books, fans, screens, furniture *(page 137)*. Every fashion, from *fêtes galantes* to pastorals, at once found its most sparkling expression in his work. One season, paper puppets were the rage; Boucher painted paper puppets.

And always there was the charming but exigent Marquise, whose greatest enjoyment was to purchase and commission works of art with a prodigality that made the people of Paris grumble. Was it not rumored that she had paid the celebrated cabinetmaker Migeon the fantastic sum of 3,000 livres for a toilet seat?

Pompadour showered Boucher with requests. One day it would be a set of pornographic pictures for the King. Another time it was a Holy Family for the Queen's private chapel. It was through this picture perhaps that Boucher's favorite model, Louise O'Murphy *(page 131)*—who posed for the figure of the Virgin—came to the King's attention and became the first boarder at the Parc-aux-Cerfs, Louis XV's private harem at Versailles. For Pompadour herself, Boucher decorated a boudoir, and when she took up engraving it was Boucher who gave her lessons and tactfully corrected her clumsy attempts.

It was a crushing load, but Boucher had many needs. He had two daughters who were soon to marry the painters Jean-Baptiste Deshays and Pierre-Antoine Baudouin; moreover, he was generous and a spendthrift. He loved all luxuries. Like his protectress, he was an avid and discriminating collector. His apartments at the Louvre (the old royal palace had been partly turned over to recognized artists and their families) were filled with treasures, including 20 etchings by Rembrandt and works by Rubens, Tiepolo, Teniers, Ruisdael, Gainsborough; also porcelain, butterflies, rare stones and sea shells.

Positions, honors, favors, wealth—Boucher obtained every worldly reward. But he had to pay the price. Society required of its painter that he present it with a flattering image of itself. The virile century of Louis

Boucher's artistic energies were tremendous, and he poured forth a stream of drawings, paintings and engravings. For six years he was the scene designer for the Paris Opéra, for which he made such sketches as this one. He also decorated the interior of a Paris theater and designed scenery and costumes for it as well as for the Opéra-Comique.

121

XIV had wielded the sword; the frail, feminine century of Louis XV could do no more than lift a fan. Bright and light, Boucher's work is a shimmering, monumental fan thrown over the foibles of Pompadour's age, a great, pretty screen that isolated it from the tough, unsavory facts of the outside world. Out there peasants starved; on his canvases peasants were dressed like lords, played the flute and made love.

Everything in Boucher's painting is the fruit of artifice, not of reality. The lovely complexions of his damsels seem the work of cosmeticians. His cooks obviously could not fry an egg, nor could his shepherdesses tell a cow from a sheep. Nothing looks natural—least of all nature. The grass is too green, the trees are too leafy: stage grass, stage trees. Boucher fills his landscapes, his kitchens, his farms, with an overabundance of props and typical details that are meant to lend them credibility but only succeed in making them appear unreal. Like a man who says too much because he cannot find the appropriate word, Boucher makes his paintings chat and babble. "He is the most deadly enemy of silence I know," Diderot said of him. And with undisguised irritation: "I daresay this man has never known truth."

The exuberant philosopher was only partly right; the work of Boucher is pure artifice, a brilliant tissue of lies, but lies and artifice were precisely the truth of the society of Boucher's time. A generation earlier, a lady had almost been lynched in the gardens of the Tuileries because she wore too much make-up. Now, a plain appearance, an air of health were regarded as vulgar. To a friend who commented on how fresh the Duchesse de Mazarin's skin was, the Duchesse de Luxembourg replied: "Yes, fresh as meat for the butcher." Women only blushed by means of the brush. Make-up became a heavy mask. Two million pots of rouge were sold annually in France. Women—and men—smothered their hair under wigs and their wigs under a layer of silvery-white powder. This delicate operation took place in special rooms where flour was blown through the ceiling and allowed to settle gently on the patient's head; people of lesser standing had themselves powdered on the staircase or in the street.

Nature was acceptable only in a remodeled version. On his first trip to Paris, Horace Walpole was struck by the fact that the French "range and fashion their trees, and teach them to hold up their heads, as a dancing master would." Facsimiles were preferable to nature; at her Château de Bellevue the Marquise de Pompadour had a garden filled with porcelain flowers sprayed with the appropriate perfumes. Lucid as they were, the members of society knew that there was no place for truth in their midst, but they believed that one could lie with style. As Voltaire put it:

> And since to err is our plight,
> Let our lies provide delight.

It was a program that Boucher executed meticulously.

Artists who cater to prevailing fashion go out with it. Neglect (and often contempt) was to be Boucher's lot for many years after his death. Unjustly so. Even Diderot, who launched the attacks against the aging painter, admitted that there was another side to his work: "He is made to turn the heads of two sorts of people, socialites and artists."

To understand what Diderot meant, post yourself in front of *The Triumph of Venus (pages 132-133)*, or *Diana's Return from the Hunt (page 134)*; close your eyes hard, and open them again, quickly. In those first few seconds, before you have time to recognize the frivolous subject matter, you may glimpse the other side of Boucher's talent, the firmness of composition, the hard radiance of line and color. One cannot help but think of Pompadour herself, of her frigidity and of the tough, cool, solid spirit that hid behind her prettiness and celebrated smile. Tuberculosis was inexorably consuming her health—she died at 43—but she bore her illness stoically and did not allow it to affect her activities. After her death, Voltaire, the spokesman of the Encyclopedists, paid her this tribute: "She was one of us." And certainly no one had practiced more rigidly the old philosopher's precept: "I wish to give you only my happy days and to suffer incognito."

The rosy Venuses and Cupids, the silken peasants and shepherdesses barely hide the underlying structure of Boucher's work: a complex, stainless, precise mechanism. Impermeable, glacial, its forms possess an al-

LE BAIN.

De la Lettre ou du Chocolat   J'ai le cœur bien plus délicat
Que préfère Madame? Ah ma chére Justine,   Plus foible infiniment, hélas! que la poitrine.

In a curious 18th Century mixture of prudery and sensuality a wealthy lady sits in her morning bath while wearing a chemise. The caption for this engraving by Sigmund Freudenberger presents her dialogue with her maid. Offered a choice between a cup of chocolate and a letter she sighs that her heart needs sustenance more than her body.

most abstract power that we meet again in the painting of David, Ingres, Matisse and Juan Gris. True, his work is artificial, but art *is* artifice; it is superficial, but painting *is* a matter of covering surfaces with pigment. Boucher marks an important step away from the Renaissance conception of art as the mirror of the world and toward the modern notion of art as an independent force whose primary function is not to mean, but to be. A number of breathtaking oil sketches are available to prove that Boucher obeyed a master stronger than fashion, favor and frivolity: Art itself. One day, some students of Jacques-Louis David, the master of the school that dethroned Boucher, were endeavoring to please him by making disparaging remarks about the late painter of the Graces. David cut them short: "Not everybody can be a Boucher."

Not even Boucher himself. Overwork and dissipation prematurely exhausted him. The pictures of his later years were often—though by no means always—repetitive and uninspired. Like onetime beauties seeking to compensate for the passing of years, they began to wear, so to speak, more and more make-up. Boucher's critics deplored the occasional harshness of his colors; even the artist admitted it, attributing this flaw to his dimming eyesight. The criticisms, whispered or trumpeted, pained him; he knew no more how to take blows than how to deal them.

His kindliness was proverbial. In 1747, the Academy had organized a competition to distribute six prizes among its 11 most distinguished members; the best picture was to obtain the biggest reward, and so on. Although Boucher's entry was certain to win, he proposed that the six prizes be pooled and split evenly among the contestants. He also stood up for principle. The candidacy of the painter Joseph-Marie Vien had twice been rejected by the Academy, whose Boucherized taste resented the new note of austerity struck by the young man. Boucher, however, looked at the picture submitted by Vien and announced that if Vien were not admitted he would never set foot in the Academy again. And it was to Vien that he later sent for instruction his young friend David, whose talent he recognized despite David's opposition to everything he himself stood for. His modesty equaled his generosity. He turned down the highly prized job of Director of the Academy's School on the ground that he had nothing to teach, that "he could only advise, brush in hand."

Boucher was made only for happiness. Age hurt him more than criticism. In 1765, about to be named First Painter to the King, he was introduced to Louis XV, who had never seen him and could not hide his astonishment at finding him older than his paintings had led him to believe. "The honor that Your Majesty has bestowed upon me will restore my youth," replied Boucher. It did not. "He had long had the air of a ghost and was afflicted by all the infirmities that come inevitably from a life consumed by work and by dissoluteness," reported Baron Grimm to a correspondent. Sorrow, to which he was not accustomed, precipitated his decline. His protectress, the Marquise de Pompadour, died in 1764; Deshays and Baudouin, his sons-in-law, died. An old, tired man, abandoned by fashion, alone amidst his collections, he went on working as one walks in one's sleep. On the morning of May 30, 1770, François Boucher was found dead in his studio—in front, so it was said, of his easel.

What happens when Boucher's kind of painting is painted by others becomes only too clear if one looks at the work of contemporaries such as Charles Natoire or Carle Van Loo, or at their disciples and imitators. It is like being in a mannequin factory, smothered under layers of roses —artificial roses—surrounded by acres of decorative canvases, screens and panels, all of them soft, mawkish and made-up like old coquettes.

Even worse was another tendency derived from Boucher's version of genre painting as practiced by artists like his own son-in-law, Pierre-Antoine Baudouin: small canvases in which Boucher's implicit lasciviousness becomes explicit. They depict scenes so private that the spectator feels he is peeping through a keyhole. One of Baudouin's most popular pictures, called *Disappointed Expectations*, shows a couple of disheveled lovers. The girl's exasperated remark is described on the engraved print that was made from the painting: "What! Is that all you can do?" We are also treated to the coyness of a lady's wedding night, to a wife's indiscretion, to provocative attitudes, oglings, *faux pas*, varying degrees of undress, lovers hastily climbing into closets or diving under beds. It is easy to understand why an engraving reproducing one such piece of naughtiness bore in its margin this annotation by the print dealer: "Not to be displayed in the show-window." Engraving and etching, whose vogue was never greater, catered to this unbuttoned taste and have done much to establish in the eyes of posterity a certain image of the age of Pompadour and of "French love."

The 18th Century was not only the age of enlightenment and refined sensibility; it was also an age of super-heated sentimentality. Even the death of the family dog might become an occasion of tearful woe and grief. The self-conscious passion for weeping and the exaggerated fashion of keeping pets reached absurd heights in ornate funerary monuments, such as this one carved by the sculptor Clodion for a beloved pet.

MUSÉE COGNACQ-JAY, PARIS

There is something frivolous and petty about this image; and it must be admitted that it was an epoch in which petty motives, small talents and diminutive artistic creations thrived. Baudouin was accepted into the Academy as a painter of miniatures. One might say that this was a perfect characterization of the trifling nature of his work. Indeed this was the age of miniatures, of fans, *bonbonnières*, music boxes and every manner of bagatelle. For the subjects of Louis XIV, the cabinetmaker Boulle had built furniture as grand as temples; for Pompadour's contemporaries Pierre Migeon and Charles Cressent made furniture *"de fantaisie"*—tiny tables for your jewelry or the-things-in-your-pockets, for sewing, for drinking coffee. "Every year," noted Voltaire, "we lavish more work and invention on our snuffboxes and similar trifles than the English on conquering the seas." No wonder that he felt he was living "in a century where everything seems a bit *petit*."

Of this pettiness, one striking illustration is the sudden vogue of pets. The previous age kicked dogs or cats when they dared to venture in from street, courtyard or kitchen. Now they were permitted to jump onto the most august laps. Louis XV had a huge angora cat, which he was forever caressing. Few are the portraits of Pompadour in which one of her favorite dogs, Innès or Mimi, is not seen playing in her skirts or cavorting on her table. One of them is immortalized by a funeral monument executed by the talented sculptor Clodion, while the greatest sculptor of the time, Jean-Antoine Houdon, carved a tomb for a bird, with the epitaph: "Here lies Fifi." Everything from château to sword thus tended to become cute and small. Chamfort, the bitter epigram writer, tells us why: "Society makes people small." And this was *the* age of social life.

The Invention
of Fashion

As the powerful, masculine figure of Louis XIV had
dominated the early years of the 18th Century, so the
equally powerful figure of Woman came to rule its
later decades. Society's attention shifted from divine
monarchy to divine femininity; fashions, crazes, vogues
held the day. The causes for the change were many: after
the Sun King's death, the Regent shook up court life
with a period of debauchery. When Louis XV took over
he proved a listless leader and he allowed his mistress,
the beautiful and intelligent Marquise de Pompadour,
to become the queen of taste and art. The poetic
Watteau, who had remained aloof from the fashions of
his own time, unwittingly set the style of the new era
with his elegant and graceful *fêtes galantes*.

The new age craved a mirror; it was a time of
portraits. But the new interest in personality, in the wit
and intelligence of the sitter finally turned into a
conventional sameness—the mask of artifice was donned
by all. Surface effects dominated art and the demand was
for decorative, delicately colored paintings, pretty little
objects, dazzling décor. Most of the artists who painted
such light decorations as the portrait at right have been
forgotten, but one man, François Boucher, rose above the
role of flatterer that society had laid out for him. A
skilled draftsman, engraver and designer, Boucher painted
brilliantly, and his art has lived long after the values
of that fashion-conscious age have tarnished.

Louis XV's daughter Adelaide had herself personified as Air, in keeping with the vogue for allegorical portraits. Another Princess, who failed to marry, was pictured as a Vestal Virgin.

Jean Marc Nattier: *Mme. Adelaide as Air*, 1750

127

Maurice Quentin de Latour: *Self-Portrait*, c.

Jean Marc Nattier: *Queen Marie Leczinska*, after 1748

Jean-Baptiste Perronneau: *Mme. de Sorquainville*, 1749

Jean-Baptiste Perronneau: *M. de Bastard*, 1747

The painter's aim has been to convey a carelessly self-confident mien, perfect elegance, and great distinction of feature," observed a later critic of the age of fashionable portraiture. These qualities show clearly on the faces illustrated here. The pastelist Maurice Quentin de Latour *(left)* pictured himself as elegantly as he did his sitters. He had good reason; his career was a fabulous success, he was accepted in society and was even asked to paint a portrait of the King. But he also painted lesser folk—at least those who could afford his high fees—with the same stylishness.

The portrait of the Queen *(above, left)* shows how fashion caused a democratization of 18th Century life. She insisted upon posing for the painter Nattier not in regal robes but in street dress. It is an unusually modest piece of royal portraiture; the dowager beside Her Majesty *(above, right)* is pictured with every bit as much elegance. The painter of this portrait, Jean-Baptiste Perronneau, was Latour's rival for a time, but his less flattering style was not so well appreciated by the modish folk of Paris. He found his clientele among the townspeople and pictured them, like the gentleman shown at right, with good-humored directness.

Boucher: *Portrait of the Artist in His Studio*

Of all the French painters of the mid-18th Century, Boucher probably expresses the taste of his time best. His skillfully painted youthful self-portrait *(left)* betrays a fluid brush and a careful attention to charming detail. Boucher was trained as an engraver and an illustrator, and one of his early assignments, a job that provided splendid lessons, was to engrave a series of Watteau drawings.

But it was not Watteau, nor the classical art that he studied during a sojourn in Rome, that stimulated Boucher most. It was his own sensual nature and his exuberant delight in women. A chief inspiration was his lovely wife, who served as his model for many years.

Boucher: *Mme. Boucher,* 1743

Boucher's portrait of her *(below, left)* shows her coyly perched on a chaise, clad in a frilly lace bodice with the fluffiest of threefold sleeves. The casual disorder of the scene, the intimate objects lying about, Mme. Boucher's suggestive smile, all are characteristics of the decorative flair that Boucher brought to his paintings. Almost totally lacking in psychological depth—Boucher's faces are often doll-like and vacuous—these pictures delighted the ladies and the gentlemen of his age. Mme. Boucher also posed for mythological paintings, sometimes portraying Venus *(pages 132-133)*, one of Boucher's favorite goddesses.

Another beauty under whose spell Boucher fell was the Marquise de Pompadour, the King's mistress. He became her protégé—receiving many commissions from her—her friend and her confidant. She became so interested in art through Boucher that she took lessons from him and became a passable engraver. But she was principally interested in keeping the King amused and she enlisted Boucher's aid. He painted erotic scenes for private Palace apartments, designed costumes for court theatricals and he did the King one special favor; he painted his own favorite model with such verve, with such wet-lipped delight that the King installed the young lady in his harem. She was Louise O'Murphy, whose charms Boucher immortalized.

Boucher: *Reclining Girl*, 1752

Boucher's favorite themes were mythological, probably because the subject gave freest rein to his passion for painting the female nude. Some 50 Venuses and countless Dianas, nymphs and Muses flowed from his brush. Boucher was not interested in mythology as it had inspired Rubens, Titian and Poussin; he merely used it to cloak his basic purpose.

His dazzling technical skill comes into full play in these works. Here, a covey of cupids draws away the curtain of night—a magical swirl of pink and silver drapery. Venus and the naiads are like pearls, contrasting sharply with the scaly, monstrous fish that carry them along. The men are muscular, with a Bacchic sensuality in their faces. The cherubs, with their golden curls, their wide eyes and dimpled thighs, are perhaps the most pinchable imps ever painted. Sheer, overwhelming sensuous joy is Boucher's message.

Boucher's spirit was little appreciated in the stricter moral climate that took over France during the Revolution. But the 19th Century historians, Edmond and Jules de Goncourt, rescued him from neglect. His secret, they noted, was his understanding of "the indiscreet pose, the coquetry of relaxed postures, the provocations of Nonchalance reclining full-length against a background of mythological apotheosis as though upon the carpet of a harem!"

Boucher: *The Triumph of Venus*, 1740

Boucher: *Leda and the Swan,* 1741

Boucher: *Diana's Return from the Hunt,* 1745

Boucher's friends compared his colors to "rose petals floating in milk." And the mythical scenes shown here demonstrate why. He had adopted the settings but not the vigorous palettes of previous painters of mythology. He used the soft tints of the boudoir, for which, indeed, many of his paintings were destined. Legend apparently meant less to him than the subtle curving of a thigh or the swell of a breast. In his drawings too, Boucher seems to capture even the reflection of blood beneath the skin, the shadow of each dimple, the line of a hip.

Boucher: Seated nude, c. 1738

Boucher: *An Autumn Pastoral*, 174

After Boucher: *Two Nymphs Surprised by a Swan*

The paintings that Boucher tossed off so prolifically perfectly fitted the new taste in décor for French homes. It was an age of prettiness, of charming rather than functional possessions. And Boucher's inventive mythological and pastoral scenes provided a source for decorative craftsmen. The white ceramic figurine at right was based on his painting *An Autumn Pastoral*, shown at left. *Leda and the Swan (page 134)* was copied on ivory *(above, right)* by an anonymous miniaturist. The vogue for *les petits objets*—little things—led to a boom in the production of miniatures, both copies of master paintings and originals.

Furniture makers also turned to Boucher for inspiration. The secretary above, although made in the later, neoclassical style, encloses a porcelain plaque that is a copy of a Boucher painting.

The Grape-Eaters, 1752

137

Boucher: Lady with an umbrella

In addition to pastorals and mythological subjects, Boucher both exploited and helped popularize a third major vogue of his day, the passion for *chinoiserie*. He incorporated Oriental objects in his paintings—for example the squatting Buddha figurine and the Chinese teapot in the bric-a-brac shelf behind Mme. Boucher on page 130—and actually painted scenes of Chinese life although he had never been to China. Oriental scenes found their way onto many popular decorative objects, screens, fans—the Boucher sketch above may have been for a fan—embroidered fabrics, and, in their grandest form, on tapestries *(right)*. Boucher was an experienced tapestry designer and made cartoons for the Beauvais factory, where he subsequently became Director, and for the Gobelins factory whose Chief Inspector he became in 1755. His inventive hand and restless creativity left distinctive marks upon his age.

Tapestry after a design by Boucher: *The Chinese Fair*

VII

Society's Many Faces

Watteau the solitary had foreseen it: the 18th Century loved nothing so much as company. Being alone was the worst calamity that could befall one. When Mme. du Deffand, who had just lost her dearest friend, made her customary appearance at the house of Mme. Marchais, who was "at home" after seven o'clock, she explained with a sigh of relief rather than sorrow: "Alas! He died at six o'clock; otherwise, you would not see me here." In Watteau's dream world, enchanted parks were the scene of fashionable gatherings. In reality the scene was the drawing room, whose Rococo mirrors saw to it that even one person alone had company. It was the great age of salons.

More than a place, a salon was an institution. It usually centered around a woman who, on a regularly appointed day of the week, threw her house open to the most brilliant, elegant, beautiful, fashionable, well-born or well-bred people she could attract. There were dozens of salons in Paris, and competition between them was often severe. Each had—or at least tried to have—a special tone, a character of its own. Some were famed for the exquisite quality of their suppers; others for the bad quality of their food. Mme. Geoffrin always served the same menu—omelette, chicken, spinach—but this lack of imagination did not prevent every important writer and philosopher from attending her dinners on Wednesdays and every well-known artist and art lover from being her guest on Mondays. Mme. Marchais' dinners, to which invitations were avidly sought, always ended with fruit from the King's private gardens, a specialty that earned her the nickname of Pomona, after the Roman goddess of fruit trees. The Duc and Duchesse de Choiseul held evening suppers for up to 80 guests, whereas the Prince de Conti, at whose mansion the young Mozart played the clavichord, gave informal teas in the English fashion, with servants replaced by lady guests who donned aprons for the occasion.

Under Louis XIV, artists had been regarded at best as high-grade valets; in the salons of the Regency and Louis XV, the aristocracy of blood and the aristocracy of the mind met on equal footing.

The Encyclopedists—so named because they collaborated on the *En-*

Concentrating intensely, a young man blows soap bubbles while a child peers over the window sill. The artist, best known for still lifes, painted people with the same sense of quiet order with which he depicted objects.

Chardin: *Soap Bubbles*, c. 1731-1733

141

cyclopédie, that monumental compendium of free-thinking in which the French Revolution was later to gather much of its ideological ammunition—were among the most highly prized attractions of the salons of the day. Indeed, all Paris seemed like a huge salon, a great hive in which human bees convened to distill that human honey, conversation. People were the only thing people were really interested in.

This was the century *par excellence* of portraits. No pre-photography epoch has left a more complete record of what its men and women looked like. Many successful painters were portraitists.

First, both in time and in celebrity, came Hyacinthe Rigaud and Nicolas de Largillière. Born in 1659, Rigaud had come to Paris from his native Provence. Le Brun had quickly guessed his talent as a portraitist and urged him to specialize in this genre. In 1688, Monsieur, the brother of Louis XIV, had himself painted by Rigaud; the painter's career was made. Twice Louis XIV posed for him. Certainly nobody was more likely to do him justice. There is something noble, solemn and majestic about all of Rigaud's portraits. Stately stance and pompous trappings lend an air of grandeur even to mediocre models. One day a fellow artist named Grimou visited him in tatters. "Monsieur Grimou," said Rigaud, "we should be delighted to enjoy your company often, but we beg you to dress a bit more properly." The next time Grimou came in better clothes and was received better. The time after he was dressed still more richly and was welcomed still more warmly. The following time, however, he returned wearing tatters; Rigaud was furious. "Sir," said Grimou, "I thought that you cultivated my acquaintance for the sake of my talents, not of the richness of my clothes. I see I was mistaken." The story is a parable of Rigaud's artistic method: clothes, he thought, made the man. He drowned his figures in heavy, sweeping cascades of cloth—veritable hyperbolas of velvet.

Although Rigaud lived until 1743, he remained a man of the preceding century. The new lightness, frivolity and artificiality were alien to him—which is perhaps the reason that he painted men better than women. To a heavily made-up lady who reproached him with not having rendered the freshness of her complexion, he replied: "How astonishing! My red paint comes from the same dealer as yours."

Largillière was three years older than Rigaud, but he was better adjusted to the new times. Unlike his rival, he preferred to depict women. His portraits are more relaxed than Rigaud's, more flexible, brighter in color. Courtly stiffness gives way to bourgeois informality. Rigaud's models look priceless; Largillière's look merely expensive. Even so, Largillière, who outlived Rigaud by three years, remains a typical subject of Louis XIV. He lacks the sprightliness that characterizes the minds and bodies of the subjects of Louis XV. His ladies are immobilized by the weight of their clothes and by their embonpoint. They are dowagers who look kindly on the agitation of the younger folk but cannot themselves take part in their frolics.

On the other hand, the women painted by Jean Marc Nattier—he painted no men to speak of—obviously can participate in the fun. If dress makes the man, undress, Nattier reasoned, makes the woman. But how could one possibly undress a nonprofessional model in public? Nattier's vogue stemmed largely from the fact that he found the solution; he cast the noble ladies of the court as goddesses and nymphs who, as everybody knew, wore—if anything at all—crowns of flowers and the shortest of tunics. The contrast between the models' respectability and their libertine attitudes, as between the glittering blue of silk folds and the pink of female faces, lent piquancy to these semi-imaginary portraits. Propriety was toyed with but preserved.

Rigaud one day complained about the difficulties of painting a woman: if you make her too beautiful, she won't recognize herself, if you show her as she is, she will be furious. Here again, Nattier found a remarkably clever solution. The faces he shows us are unabashedly made up, prettified and so stereotyped as to be almost interchangeable. But that was precisely why all women recognized themselves in Nattier's flattering mirror. Fashion imposed—then as now—an artificial, idealized mask that was adopted by all and that, as a result, made them all look alike. Nattier's ingenious formula was precisely what Louis XV's homely daughters needed, and he became the official portraitist of the royal family (*pages 126-127*). This distinction set off a chain reaction of commissions on all sides. If the King's daughters could be made to look graceful, more than one woman unconsciously reasoned, anybody could. Nattier fully deserved his great popularity: he had perhaps not painted great works of art, but he had squared the circle.

To find the true image of society in the age of Pompadour, we must turn to the pastels by Maurice Quentin de Latour. Truth had always been Latour's prime concern. At the twilight of his life he wrote to an acquaintance: "I still love truth, which shall forever be the idol of my soul." The countless portraits which he executed during his long career (he lived from 1704 to 1788) testify to this idolatry. Here, breathtaking, lifelike, are the men and women who animated the salons of 18th Century France: poised, alert, nimble of body and of mind, elegant, affable—social animals in all their glory. "*Che figure interessanti!*" as

The salon, an institution almost as powerful as the royal court, developed during the mid-18th Century under the guidance of fashionable and well-educated ladies. The one pictured here was typical of festive occasions at which members of "good society"—the social and intellectual elite —met to chat, gossip and witness entertainments. The salons represented a leveling of society—marquises mixed with merchants—that was to end the dominance of the court over French life.

Don Giovanni would have said—what interesting faces! Their mobile features exude wit. Their eyes sparkle with the excitement of ideas (Latour refused, whenever possible, to portray stupid people)—ideas that they are eager to communicate. They are taut, tuned like stringed instruments ready, at the slightest solicitation, to emit the sound of conversation. From within their frames they greet us with the barely repressed elation of people whom solitude has condemned to silence and who at last espy an interlocutor. Sometimes an almost imperceptible smile plays on the thin lips, parted as if about to utter a *bon mot*, impatient to display a talent for repartee. Looking at these portraits, we are reminded of the innumerable thrusts and parries from that unending verbal fencing match known as *la vie de société.*

The illusion of reality is staggering—and was to his contemporaries. Latour himself tells how a man once asked him to paint his portrait and to frame it in such a way that it would seem a mirror. Then, while his wife slept, he substituted the portrait for the mirror on her dressing table. Next morning, when she glanced in it, the effect was so convincing that she turned around, thinking her husband stood behind her. And Latour adds: "I supposed he was an Englishman; what Frenchman would have acted thus?" For once he was too modest. Every civilized Frenchman recognized himself and his friends in Latour's magic mirror. Hence his fabulous popularity.

Like Watteau, Latour was born in the north of France, at Saint-Quentin, and had to overcome parental resistance—his father was a musician—to become a painter. Like Watteau, too, he ran away to Paris to learn his trade. An obscure engraver named Tardieu gave him his first lessons. Little is known about these beginnings, except that he went to England for a short time and upon his return presented himself as an English painter, a trick that earned him commissions from snobs afflicted with Anglomania.

Once, in those early days, he executed a group of portraits for the family of the painter Louis de Boullongne. The latter examined them and shouted: "Look, you unhappy fellow, and tell me if you are worthy of the gift Nature gave you. Draw and keep drawing, if you want to become a man!" Latour followed the advice scrupulously; he kept drawing till the end, and practically never took up the brush again. Pastel became his medium. It was ideally suited to the times. Its delicate powderings and smearings were the exact artistic counterpart of the powders and smears that composed the make-up on the faces of socialite sitters. Pastel, too, was a gentlemanly medium. "It does not dirty one's hands and stain one's clothes, like oil paint," a distinguished writer on art explained. Such considerations were important for an artist who wished to move in a society where sculptors were not easily accepted because the sloppy clay with which they worked branded them as manual laborers.

Latour ran no such risk; for him, artistic and worldly success went hand in hand. He was a regular at the most exclusive salons. Writers like Fontenelle and Duclos, mathematicians such as D'Alembert, philosophers like Rousseau were his friends. Voltaire invited him to Ferney, his residence. All appreciated the fire of his conversation although they

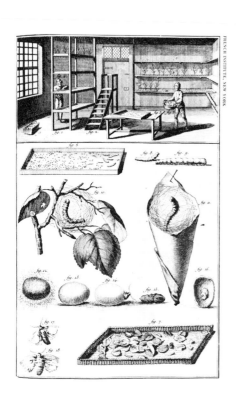

This page from Diderot's famous encyclopedia depicts the making of silk. That extraordinary work, in 35 volumes, edited by Denis Diderot with the help of some 180 experts, attempted to survey the total knowledge of mankind and was of enormous influence in shaping the minds of the men who made the French Revolution, and, indeed, the modern world.

were not blind to a certain confusion that reigned in his mind. In true socialite fashion, he dabbled in astronomy—had not Voltaire complained that ladies now spent their nights in the park not to listen to love declarations but to level telescopes at the stars? He took up mathematics, ethics, metaphysics and even began to learn Latin at the age of 55. He himself played host to the witty, the wise and the wealthy at his Paris house or in his suburban villa. And of course, like a true man of the world, he had taken a famous prima donna as his mistress.

After his 80th birthday his devoted brother took him back to Saint-Quentin. A reception worthy of a monarch—church bells ringing, guns firing, banners, fanfares, speeches, crowds—awaited him on his arrival. There he spent his last years, endowing charitable funds, lost in humanitarian-pantheistic dreams. When at last senility befuddled his brain he spent his time talking to trees and plants on his rambles through the countryside, proclaiming that only the Emperor of Russia was richer than he. In 1788, on the eve of the political cataclysm that swept away the society he had portrayed, he died, kissing the hands of his servants.

Yet Latour was not really a happy man. He was susceptible, irritable, tormented to an unusual degree. The cause of his dissatisfaction was in his work. As he wrote to one of his models, "All is lost in my pastel when I fall prey to a moment that differs from the given one; unity is destroyed." Light, atmosphere and expression change continually. In his desperate pursuit of the moment of truth, Latour submitted his sitters to long, gruelling hours of posing—and then often destroyed his work in the end. Or, in his later years, he would spoil it in the effort to fix the butterfly-wing delicacy of pastel tones.

But there was a still deeper reason for his frustration than this technical one. The clue is provided by Latour's behavior toward his patrons. It was downright impossible. His models were exposed to sarcasm, abrupt changes of humor, impertinence. He charged an old friend an exorbitant price for her portrait because she did not share his views on music. He proclaimed that the rich should pay for the poor. When a financier sent a valet to inform the artist that he could not come for his umptieth sitting, Latour said to the servant: "I like your head better, anyway; I shall do *your* portrait." Pompadour got into trouble with him. He had agreed to portray her, provided no one entered her room while he worked; the King did; Latour left in a rage. He refused to complete the portraits of the King's daughters because they had made him wait, and finally the King himself fell afoul of his bad temper. Louis XV had come to pose for him in a room which did not suit the artist, who protested angrily. "I thought we would be less disturbed here," the King ruefully explained. "I did not know that Your Majesty was not the master in his own house," Latour replied.

All these eccentricities were the symptoms of the artist's profound resentment against the society that posed for him. Latour idolized truth —unique, individual truth. He regarded himself as a kind of Diogenes at the court of Louis XV. "My models believe that I capture only their features, but I plumb the innermost depths of their personalities without their being aware of it, and carry them off complete." Yet when we look at Latour's gallery of portraits, we are struck by their kinship—their monotony, one is almost tempted to say. All those faces look at us with the same eyes, smile at us with the same smile. Far from revealing people's innermost being, they display standardized graces: the same superficial politeness, skin-deep vivacity, shallow brightness. They are faces shaped by and for social intercourse; inner life is either dried up or out of reach. This is what defeated Latour. He sought truth, but his models were cogs in the intricate machinery of social life and their truth was artifice. The mirror did not lie; the face that it showed did. The wife of the Président de Rieux, in Latour's portrait, has taken off her mask; yet her face, smooth as her dress, is an even more impenetrable mask.

Thus it was *le beau monde* that made Latour's work artificial. The work of his younger, less popular rival, Jean-Baptiste Perronneau is less so. Lacking the choice patronage available in Paris, Perronneau traveled through the provinces and abroad—he usually had the town drummer announce his arrival and his prices—accepting whoever would pay him. His subjects were mostly solid, unprepossessing burghers or country squires, whose straightforwardness is mirrored in Perronneau's robust, abrupt art. He was a bolder, freer painter than Latour and, in a sense, more interesting to the modern eye. "I did some vigorous things at Abbeville," he says in a letter; he could not have done them in Paris or at Versailles.

Latour sensed that he was a slave to society. His eccentricities were protests against this bondage. But society loved him the more for his eccentricities. "My talent belongs to me," he boasted, but society knew better; his self-portrait is indistinguishable from all his other portraits. His talent, dazzling as it was, remained a social talent, a brilliant form of conversation. It lacked the one quality that allows art to reach the greatest heights, the quality which Watteau possessed superlatively and whose absence Diderot so bitterly deplored in Boucher: silence.

A miraculous respite is provided in the mad whirl of 18th Century painting by Jean-Baptiste Siméon Chardin. He was a painter of still lifes, or rather, of the still life, and his work is in contrast to the agitation of social life that made Chamfort say about the Parisianized David Hume: "He must be dead: I saw him only three times today."

Chardin was born in 1699, the oldest child of a cabinetmaker who specialized in billiard tables. The atmosphere in the Chardin home can easily be imagined: one of modest tradespeople, who by dint of hard work had risen from plebeian rank to bourgeoisie. The glitter of society had not penetrated their sphere. Honor was a concern for nobles; honesty was the virtue cherished in the bourgeois world. It was not a brilliant but a serious world, unimaginative but painstakingly scrupulous, thrifty but dependable, patient and sound, a world of wool rather than silk. In it, things—from a dress to a marriage—were made to be used and to last. Suits, household utensils and furniture were handed down from generation to generation, as were professional secrets. The horizon was narrow, but what fell within its scope was known intimately.

Fame and fortune were to come to Chardin, yet to the end he remained a typical representative of his class. He was a plain man, sober, stocky and robust, who never overcharged for his canvases but was almost exasperatingly careful with his money. He was honest and fair (the Academy made him its treasurer and entrusted him with the ticklish task of hanging the Salons). He was an orderly and neat man who asked to be shaved even while on his deathbed. He was as secretive about his technique (nobody ever saw him paint) as a chef about his pet recipes. He was chary of words but filled with good sense. In him the qualities, attitudes and outlook of the little people, discreet to the point of silence, find their most accomplished spokesman.

When the cabinetmaker's son expressed his desire to become a painter, his father was not upset. For him, painting was not an art but a craft, like carpentry, and his ideas about learning it were correspondingly down-to-earth. Prix de Rome? French Academy? He never thought of them. When young Chardin timidly expressed the wish to learn the humanities, Chardin *père* flatly rejected the idea as unnecessary. The boy was apprenticed to a mediocre painter named Pierre-Jacques Cazes, in whose workshop he copied pictures much as Watteau had on the Pont Notre-Dame. He displayed sufficient talent to be accepted as an apprentice by Noël-Nicolas Coypel. One day, it is said, his employer asked him to paint the gun in the portrait of a huntsman. That is how Chardin encountered the genre of which he was to become the greatest exponent: the still life.

In the hierarchy of the genres that the century of Louis XV had inherited from the century of Louis XIV, the historic, heroic or religious narrative was the aristocrat; the still life was the commoner, and was remunerated accordingly. For years Chardin led a difficult existence, although some collectors were buying his paintings. Better days seemed ahead when he became engaged to a girl from a slightly higher layer of the bourgeoisie. Unfortunately her family was financially ruined, probably in the sequel of Law's bankruptcy. It was enough to cancel the wedding (indeed Chardin *père* advised this course); but the young painter remained loyal to his oath and married his impoverished fiancée.

By the time of his marriage Chardin had already attracted the attention of connoisseurs at the yearly open-air exhibitions on the Place Dauphine. They urged him to seek admission into the Academy, and in 1728 he submitted several canvases. He placed them against a wall and stood away. The illustrious Largillière came in, looked at them and pronounced them to be the work of a good Flemish painter. When the young artist told him the truth, Largillière offered to become his sponsor. Chardin was accepted and admitted on the same day under the label: "Skilled in animals and fruit."

It was by no means a new skill; Largillière himself was an eminent practitioner of it. His flamboyantly arranged *buffets garnis* are the pompous and contrived equivalents of his formal portraits. Nature it was, but as a major-domo in a four-star restaurant would conceive it. The hunting trophies by François Desportes, quasi-official portraitist of hounds to His Majesty Louis XIV, are no less bombastic. One of Chardin's chief competitors, Jean-Baptiste Oudry, occasionally presents objects more simply but not more naturally. They are chosen for their decorative effect.

Oudry plays on a hare's coat as Paganini played on his violin—for effect. The plumages of his ducks are as brilliant and cold as Nattier's silks.

But Chardin absorbed little from these men. His real predecessors —and Largillière's intuition had not misled him—were the Flemish and Dutch *petits maîtres*, the very same painters who also enable us to measure Chardin's unique gifts. The still lifes of the Flemish masters are unglorified, precise renditions of reality—too precise, for fish, fruit and flower are pierced by the sharp attention of the painter as game is by the hunter. They have become objects of mental or physical possession, material for study or food for the table. They are in the strictest sense *nature morte*, "dead nature," the French term for still life.

Chardin is the first and practically the only artist who substituted still life for dead nature. So bewitchingly true are his peaches or strawberries that the desire to eat them would strike the spectator as a form of cannibalism. One could no more bring oneself to do it than one could slaughter a rabbit after allowing it to become a pet, a familiar. And that is just what the objects in Chardin's still lifes are: familiars, old friends. "Be gentle, Sirs, be gentle," he once mildly admonished some fiery acquaintances. So gentle, so peaceful is he with things and creatures, so accustomed have they become to him—for years, we meet them again and again, mellowed and patinaed by time, the copper cistern, the stone pitcher, the pipe *(pages 151-155)*—that they relax, relinquishing the attitude of frozen silence with which they protect themselves from the rest of us. To Chardin they consent to show themselves as they are when we are not disturbing or paralyzing them by looking. The intimate whisper that seems to rise from their innermost depths and, as it reaches the surface, turns into the fragile velvet of a peach's skin or the savorous texture of a plum or the luminous halo of a plate—that whisper is the very sound of nature's life.

Chardin's contemporaries recognized his mastery. But they regarded him as merely the greatest practitioner of what, to them, was still the lowest—and therefore the cheapest—kind of painting. This discrimination irritated Chardin. One day, the story goes, his friend the painter Jacques-André Joseph Aved told him he had declined the commission of a portrait because only 400 livres had been offered for it. "But that is a great deal of money," exclaimed Chardin. "You must think that portraits are as easy to paint as sausages," Aved replied. Peeved, Chardin turned to figures; between 1737 and 1752 he ceased exhibiting (and perhaps painting) still lifes.

In a way he did paint his figures like his sausages. Everything is tranquil, almost silent in his scenes of life at home. Mother and daughter, governess and little boy understand each other without uttering a word: a brief exchanged glance is enough. An exquisite complicity characterizes their relationship, as it does that of the maid to her pail. All is hushed, quietly concentrated. Action is either suspended or requires so much delicacy, patience and stillness as to verge on immobility. And again, from candid children, honest housewives and placid servants rises the subtle whisper—so thrillingly close to silence—of life.

In an age of artifice nothing seems as unnatural as the natural. People believed that Chardin had a secret way of painting, a magic trick—did he not hide when he worked? It was rumored that he used his thumb as much as his brush, that he had colors of which he alone knew the formula. Certainly Chardin applied his pigments as nobody but Rembrandt had ever done. His strokes were juxtaposed abruptly, without transitions—critics were reminded of mosaics and noted that his compositions "jelled" only at a distance—yet they are tightly bound together, subtly and inextricably interwoven. Never before, furthermore, had texture played so considerable a role in easel painting; from veil-like lightness to masonrylike thickness, from smooth to rough, Chardin commanded an apparently inexhaustible scale of densities. No wonder critics thought his secret lay in his technical skill.

But he knew better. To an artist who shared the prevailing opinion about him, he said: "But who told you that one painted with colors?" "With what else?" the other asked in astonishment. "One uses colors but one paints with feelings," Chardin replied. Feeling, however, can be as oppressive as indifference. Chardin's feeling never weighs down nor pushes his models. Just as gentleness restrains his power, tact controls his sentiments. That is where his seemingly dominant concern with technique comes in. For things and creatures to feel at home and natural, one must mind one's own business; Chardin's business was pigments and brushes, and in attending to it he produced peaceful paintings. In them an almost Edenlike atmosphere, a sense of tranquil coexistence, marks the relationship between matter and manner.

His own time did not really fathom these mysteries. His success was based, at least partly, on a misunderstanding. "Chardin: animals, natural things, little naive subjects"—so he is listed among the best painters in the Academy. He was regarded as the French Teniers. "I would give ten Watteaus for a Teniers," said Diderot, revealing that Chardin's popularity was not so much his own but of genre painting in general.

It was a fragile basis for prosperity. With age Chardin gradually fell out of fashion. Had his second wife—the first died in 1735, leaving him a son—not been a model of thriftiness, he might have relapsed into the straitened circumstances of his youth. He had always been a slow worker; in his late years he almost ceased to paint. Sorrow and discomfort assailed him. His son, a less than mediocre painter, died mysteriously in Venice. Chardin suffered from kidney stones and the other infirmities of extreme old age. His whole career, however, had been a demonstration of how to turn limitations into achievements; these ultimate handicaps led him to artistic triumphs: his pastel portraits of his wife and of himself (*pages 160-161*). He who had never drawn switched from brush and knife to pastel.

Tact is not called for when one looks into the mirror. These final self-portraits are almost brutal in the abruptness of their execution. Life reduced to its strict minimum is captured by an art reduced to its essence. Light has gone out of the eyes, color has deserted the flesh. All is covered by ashes. Only one ember remains burning, red-hot: the stick of pastel in the artist's hand. These works—less than a handful survive—were done as late as 1779. At the end of that year, Chardin died.

This sketch, entitled *Fox with a Dead Partridge*, is by Jean-Baptiste Oudry, who was the official "portrait painter of the royal hounds." Oudry and the painter François Desportes made fine careers for themselves with realistic animal paintings, but few artists followed them and the genre gradually died out. Oudry's sketches are treasured by art lovers among sportsmen.

A World in Harmony

Jean-Baptiste Siméon Chardin, master painter of still life and scenes of domestic tranquillity, remained aloof from the artistic sophistications of his time and created a hushed and harmonious world of glowing color. He came of age in the 1720s, soon after the untimely death of Watteau, and he has been ranked as the greatest glory in French art between Watteau and the Revolution. The work shown at right, wrapped in the luminous stillness that pervades each of his pictures, helps to explain why. The objects themselves are all quite ordinary—a water cistern, a ladle, a bucket, a jug—but Chardin's treatment of them is unique. Who else in his time would have dared such a simple composition, unburdened with anecdotal details and free from any mere display of virtuosity? Who understood so well the soft diffusion of natural light, the well-tuned composure of a carefully delimited space? Whose textures are so rich, so varied; whose colors interact so perfectly?

Chardin had the ability to make an old crock as lovely as a jewel and could breathe an almost human life into a piece of ripe fruit. But Chardin's remarkable technique never intrudes: his still lifes and genre scenes are so disarmingly modest that, as the Encyclopedist and art critic Denis Diderot said 200 years ago: "You halt in front of a Chardin instinctively, almost without noticing it, just as a weary traveler will sit down in a spot that offers him greenery, silence, shade and water."

Objects recur in Chardin's still lifes and genre scenes with reassuring regularity. The cistern and jug seen here appear in works on pages 152 and 159. These and others were kept and lovingly painted by the artist many times.

Chardin: *The Copper Cistern*, c. 1733

150

Chardin: *The Skate*, c. 1727

Not yet 30 years old, Chardin won instant acceptance in the Royal Academy with the work above, which at first was mistaken for that of a Flemish master. Indeed, paintings like *The Skate*, with its Baroque busyness and anecdotal intrusion—the live cat snarling at oysters—owe more to Dutch and Flemish still lifes than to the crisp and decorative works of Chardin's countrymen. But even in this early painting, Chardin manifests his interest in the physical qualities of objects. Throughout his career he was absorbed in the problem of capturing those qualities in thickly applied paints that unfailingly evoke the objects themselves. In the detail at left from the work below, for example, the white areas of the pomegranate catch, bend and reflect light to give the illusion of the moist, pulpy textures of the fruit.

Chardin: *Still Life with Grapes and Pomegranates*, 1763

153

Chardin always painted from nature. He is believed to have drawn very little, preferring to develop his compositions by brushing color directly onto canvas rather than by first working them out in sketch form. The carefully placed objects in his still lifes are defined in space not by sharp outlines but by highlights which seem to bring near objects forward and by shadows that heighten the illusion of depth and shape. The magnificently balanced work shown here contains many such object lessons on Chardin's technique. The silver cup at left, for instance, is completely shaped by light. Its edges almost dissolve into soft shadow; no hard contour is to be found, and the cool, bright metal can almost be felt.

Perhaps Chardin's greatest achievement is his brilliant mastery of textures. The paintings on the preceding pages demonstrate his ability to capture the look and feel of tender animal flesh and the juiciness of ripe fruit. Here he deals with the smoothness of metals, the dry chalkiness of clay, the satiny finish of well-handled wood, the warm nap of worn velvet and the porous sheen of earthenware. As always, Chardin's brushwork is infinitely varied, and each stroke is so distinct that the forms in his paintings seem to melt when looked at closely, only to come into focus again when the viewer moves back.

Chardin's mastery of composition and his ability, like that of Vermeer, to capture both external illumination and inner radiance made his works indispensable textbooks for the painters who followed him, especially many modern artists. The solid structure of his paintings has been compared with Cézanne's. Van Gogh, noting that his tones were achieved on the surface of the canvas by an adroit juxtaposition of strokes of pure color, proclaimed him Rembrandt's equal in this respect. Matisse admired his poetry, and Picasso and Braque were impressed by his craftsmanship and unfailing sense of order.

Chardin: *Clay Pipe and Earthenware Jug*, c. 1760-1763

155

Chardin: *The House of Cards* (Portrait of M. Lenoir), c. 1741

Although he had achieved a measure of success with still lifes, selling steadily to affluent collectors, Chardin's preoccupation with the subject was considered a career handicap by his friends. Still life was regarded as a secondary field commanding low prices; an artist who limited himself to still lifes could not capitalize on the large market for engravings, which were usually based on paintings of genre subjects. A friend twitted Chardin about the relative ease of painting "sausages," and a critic condescendingly admired him for "having found the art of pleasing the eyes, even with disgusting subjects."

Whether Chardin was influenced by these opinions or simply felt the need to express himself more broadly, he eventually turned to painting people. When he did so, he did it brilliantly. The two paintings shown here illustrate the special qualities Chardin brought to this kind of picture. The figures are as carefully arranged as apples on a table; the atmosphere is stilled by their intense concentration, and Chardin's careful control of light and harmonic sense of color are vividly evident. His subjects give the impression that they share Chardin's understanding of objects.

Chardin: *Child with a Top* (Portrait of Auguste-Gabriel Godefroy), c. 1738

Chardin: *Grace Before a Meal*, c. 1740

Silence, calm and order prevail in Chardin's domestic scenes just as in his still lifes. These works, like the portraits shown on the preceding pages, are "stilled" life: Chardin never simply catches a subject in motion and arbitrarily stops him; he selects those legitimate instants when people naturally come to rest, if only fleetingly. In the picture above, it is that moment when a mother waits for her youngest child to finish saying grace before she serves the meal. At right, he senses the weary seconds when a young housewife back from market lays down her bulky round loaves of bread and gathers strength to swing her shopping bag onto the cabinet. In every picture, time is arrested and the viewer becomes momentarily but completely involved with Chardin's subject.

Chardin: *Return from Market*, 1739

159

Chardin: *Self-Portrait with Spectacles*, 1771

Chardin: *Portrait of Madame Chardin*, 1775

Chardin lived to be 80 years old, and in his later years he took up a medium that was entirely new to him. Having spent his life learning the intricacies of oil painting—he was so knowledgeable about pigments and color that the Academy frequently called upon him for advice—he now began to work in pastels, which employ the same pigments used in oil painting but are bonded together with chalk and gum into crayonlike sticks. The reason for the change is not known, but it may have been that with pastels an artist can work quickly. Chardin had always been a slow worker in oils, so slow that it was said some of his still-life subjects decayed before he could finish painting them. Pastels also require less preparation than oils, and Chardin may have found the medium more relaxing. One scholar also suggested that the old master could no longer take the strong odors given off by oil paints. Whatever his reasons, Chardin brought to pastels the same vitality that characterizes his best paintings.

The self-portraits shown here, along with one of his beloved wife, are among the finest works in pastel. Chardin has faced himself and his helpmate with honesty and directness. As the novelist Marcel Proust said of Chardin's self-portraits, "They seem to be saying half-boastfully, half-wistfully: Yes, indeed, I'm an old man now." But the old man has lost none of his vigor with color. In the portrait at left, he has laid the color down in bold strokes, juxtaposing pure tones to create the subtle forms of his aged face. Throughout this remarkable work Chardin uses dashes of pure color, often daringly unnatural—greens, blues—to create the skin tones and textures. How different his bold technique is from that of those traditional pastelists who applied carefully related approximations of flesh color like make-up. Chardin was to the end an innovator, an experimenter.

Chardin: *Self-Portrait with an Eyeshade*, 1775

A characteristic example of the
sentimental vogue is this tearful
scene in which a wounded soldier
(*right*) limps to his dying
father's side to beg forgiveness
for having run off to the wars.

VIII

A Glittering
Era Fades

Jean-Baptiste Greuze: *A Father's Curse,
the Punished Son,* 1781

At the beginning of his long reign, Louis XV was nicknamed "The Well
Loved." By the time he died, in 1774, this epithet had been replaced by
"The Ill Loved." People had grown tired not only of his depravity and
cynicism but also of the political and economic decisions of his ministers,
and even of the artistic tastes, values and fashions that are gathered today
under the labels "Style of Louis XV" and "Style of Madame Pompadour." Actually the symptoms of a new trend began to manifest themselves around the middle of the century. But for the trend to prevail it
required a catalyst, a symbol. Nations love simplification; they want to
be able to recognize themselves and their times in a single historic figure
—one that they can bury later on, if necessary and, by so doing, turn a
new page. That figure was provided at last in the shape of Louis XV's
grandson and successor, who rightfully gave his name to the style that
dominates the second half of the century: Louis XVI.

He was a man of simple tastes, moral to the point of prudishness.
No sooner was he on the throne than he ordered destroyed the libidinous
paintings executed by Boucher for Bellevue, where Louis XV and Pompadour used to seek refuge from court life.

Practically overnight sin went out of fashion and virtue became the
rage. As one man, France decided to go straight. In the architecture and
furniture of Louis XVI's age, clean, perpendicular lines replaced the sensuous curves of the Rococo. This classic—or, more precisely neoclassic
—revival drew its inspiration from a sudden renewal of interest in antiquity, sparked by the systematic diggings at Herculaneum and Pompeii
and by the eloquent re-assessment of the Greco-Roman heritage under-
taken in Rome by a German scholar, Johann Winckelmann. An Etruscan, or Pompeiian, vogue was introduced into France by the Comte de
Caylus, who, though a close friend of Watteau, fostered the austere
forms that killed the amorous arabesques spun by the master of the
fêtes galantes. Could this be the same Caylus? Not quite. Archeology
had made him acrimonious and dogmatic. He swore only by antiquity
and even asked to be buried in an imitation Roman sarcophagus, thereby prompting Diderot to write the following couplet:

163

Here lies an antiquarian whose temper was sour and hot;
How fittingly he's buried in this Etruscan pot!

After 1760, antiquity had won the day. "Its fashion has become so general," wrote Diderot's friend Grimm, "that everything today is *à la grecque*." Actors at the Comédie Française played in what they considered historically accurate costumes. Christoph Gluck's solemn *Iphigénie* chased Jean-Philippe Rameau's gallant make-believe Indians off the stage of the Opéra, prompting Voltaire to write prophetically: "Louis XVI and Gluck will create a new kind of Frenchman." Queen Marie-Antoinette, wearing a Grecian tunic and a laurel wreath, played the harp in her toy temple at the Petit-Trianon. From architecture to dress, simplicity, that eminently Roman virtue, became the password. Simultaneously with the classic vogue, a parallel trend toward the simple life was developing as a result of the philosophy of Jean-Jacques Rousseau. Rousseau held that man was naturally good and that society corrupted him. Back to the noble savage, he urged, back to the man of feeling and down with the man of ideas. No swaddling of newlyborns, he preached, no reading before the age of 12. Listening to the gospel of simple virtue preached by Rousseau and by the Encyclopedists, husbands and wives rediscovered the pleasures of parenthood. Indeed, women took their roles as mothers so seriously that they sometimes actually breastfed their babies instead of handing that task over to wet nurses.

The flamboyant and sensual Rococo style of Louis XV's era was replaced by a disciplined classicism under Louis XVI. Archeologists, then busy digging up Greek and Roman ruins in Italy and Dalmatia, played a role in this classical revival. The stand above, symmetrically carved and decorated with ormolu (gilt brass) was made in France, and reflects the new taste for an orderly décor.

THE METROPOLITAN MUSEUM OF ART, NEW YORK,
BEQUEST OF JAMES ALEXANDER SCRYMSER, 1926

In their eagerness to prove that they had soft hearts the French resorted to a new pastime: weeping. "What amused her," said Mme. de Staël about her mother, "was what made her cry." It was principally Rousseau who opened the gates to tears. In novelistic tracts, essays, and even in a pastoral operetta, he unleashed torrents of sentimentality. One of his best-known works—published in 72 editions between 1761 and 1800—was *Julie or the New Héloïse*, a romance written in the form of letters. It tells the story of a young woman who falls passionately in love with a poor young tutor but is prevented by her father from marrying him. After she is properly married to a wealthy foreigner—to whom she dutifully confesses her former indiscretion—her husband hires the tutor for his own children and the passion flares anew. But the young wife nobly suppresses her feelings for the sake of preserving her home, maintaining the honor of her family and providing her children with a good moral education. On reading Rousseau's tale of the painful pleasures of virtue, millions wept.

Fainting also became fashionable; Mme. de Lamballe earned herself a reputation for extreme sensitivity because she could hold a fainting spell for more than two hours. No pleasures were deemed more exquisite than those of melancholy.

The source of goodness was, as Rousseau told his readers, Mother Earth. One no longer "buried oneself in the country," as the preceding generation put it, but rushed to it as to the fount of life. Babies were whisked off to farms to be reared, and the cradles of especially weak ones were placed in stables so that they could benefit from the health-giving atmosphere. The peasant's life came to be regarded as the ideal one.

Mirabeau the Elder, the theoretician of the back-to-nature movement who claimed (at the dawn of the Industrial Revolution!) that only agrarian economies were sound, was hailed as "the friend of Man." Every courtier simply had to have his farm. Marie-Antoinette ordered one to be built for herself at Versailles; she called it Le Hameau and could be seen there with her ladies in waiting, milking her cows. At the Duchesse de Mazarin's Paris residence, gentlemen dressed as shepherds led a flock of beribboned sheep into the grand salon, but the ungrateful beasts wrecked it. Addressing himself to his countrymen, Voltaire could write with some justification: "Once you were monkeys that gamboled; now you want to be oxen that ruminate: the change does not suit you."

Virtue was the only fashion with which Boucher and his inferior imitators could not cope. The new age longed for a new artist—and soon found him. At the Salon of 1755 public attention was attracted by a canvas entitled *The Father of the Family Explaining the Bible to His Children*. A critic noted that it did "honor to its author's mind and heart; it is believed that he possesses a sensitive and delicate soul."

The young artist was Jean-Baptiste Greuze; and such was his success that he never swerved from the moral-sentimental path he had opened in that picture. In *The Village Bride* a venerable, hard-working father is seen on the day of the betrothal, blessing his bashful, virginal daughter. She, meanwhile, is comforted by her solid, loving mother and by her prospective husband, a good, honest boy, amidst the tears of joy shed by the grandparents, the laughter of the children and the cackling of hens—for we are in a farmer's home: Greuze liked to hold all the aces in his hand. In another of his paintings we see a majestic pater-familias cursing his no-good son, who prefers joining the army to doing useful work on the homestead. In another *(page 162)* the old sage, now paralyzed, is dying, surrounded by his despairing progeny, but the prodigal son returns just in time to obtain his begetter's forgiveness. When Greuze wants to relax from the strain of these tear-jerking parables, he turns to blushing damsels and innocent tots who mourn over a broken pitcher, a fractured mirror or a dead canary.

Everybody, from Encyclopedists to good society, exulted. At last had come the man to rescue painting from the debauchery into which Boucher and his followers had plunged it. Diderot announced enthusiastically, "Greuze is the pictorial preacher of good behavior as Baudouin is of bad behavior." His paintings teach us, correct our vices and invite us to become virtuous.

The tears that Greuze made his contemporaries shed must have blinded them to the real merits of his work. Today much of it appears heavy-handed, dull and pedestrian. Even the better part of it, the portraits, are marred by mawkishness. We have learned that garrulousness is art's worst enemy; what counts is not whether it preaches a good or a bad message but that it should not preach at all. At that, one may ask oneself whether Greuze really was as pure as he seemed. The eroticism of yore has not been banished but driven underground; it lurks perversely beneath the thin crust of morality and sentiment. We need not be Freudians to guess that Greuze's shyly blushing damsels weep not over the loss of a pet or a broken mirror but over their lost innocence.

In truth the age of Louis XVI and Marie-Antoinette could understand and accept real virtue no more than real nature. When he has tried every other disguise, Satan masquerades as an angel; similarly, nothing was more sophisticated than Louis XVI simplicity. Its sincerity was false; its tears did not wet. One day the extravagant Queen turned up with a leek, a bundle of radishes, a carrot and a cauliflower artfully disposed on her coiffure. "How marvelous!" exclaimed one of the ladies present. "Henceforth I shall wear nothing else on my head; it looks so much more natural than flowers!" The hairdo *à la gardener* was born.

That was what the age meant by "natural." So-called English or Chinese gardens now replaced French gardens, as if the former's carefully planned irregularities, their artificial waterfalls and ruins designed to stimulate melancholy were any less contrived than the formal patterns of the latter. Thus, by a curious swap, the curves—chased from the house, where straight lines now held sway—found shelter in the park. A year after Louis XV's death, Louis XVI ordered the geometrically planted and pruned old trees of Versailles to be cut down; he entrusted the painter Hubert Robert with the landscaping of the new gardens at the Petit-Trianon.

Hubert Robert needed only to transpose into reality the universe which he was already and continuously representing in his paintings: landscapes cleverly peppered with countryfolk, savage rocks, gloomy tombs and, above all, Roman monuments. Robert had spent 11 years in Italy; even after his return, he remained faithful to one recipe: "scenic" landscapes made picturesque by means of a hundred permutations and combinations of more or less fanciful Roman ruins—they earned him the nickname of "Robert of the Ruins."

Land was Robert's specialty, the sea that of his equally fashionable colleague Joseph Vernet—picturesque seas, of course, drenched in moonlight or in the rays of the rising sun. Nor was action missing. Vernet's celebrated shipwrecks provided art lovers with endless opportunities for shedding tears and experiencing the delicious thrills of terror, pity and admiration. Here were mammoth waves, dread lightning bolts, men drowning, mothers sacrificing their lives to save their children, gallant rescuers, exhausted survivors, bodies washed up on lonely shores. Today, Vernet's seascapes look stagey, as spent as last year's fireworks—cardboard tempests and tinfoil moons that could be convincing only to people who fancied that a leek as a hairdo was the epitome of naturalness.

The poison of artifice, working its insidious way, affected the judgment of all who came in contact with it. Robert and Vernet would have been genuinely surprised and distressed by the modern opinion of them. There was only one way to escape its ravages: to be an outsider, like Watteau, who came too soon, or like Chardin, who stood too low, or like Gabriel de Saint-Aubin.

Although Saint-Aubin's parents, modest tradespeople, certainly had not read Diderot's demographic appeals, they practically set off a population explosion on their own: 15 children, of whom only two girls and five boys survived. Gabriel's older brother was a designer of lace pat-

Philosopher, novelist, dramatist and art critic, Denis Diderot made a profound impact on the 18th Century. As editor of a great encyclopedia, he helped spread new ideas on science, technology and art. His later years were dogged by misfortune until he came under the patronage of Catherine the Great of Russia. On her behalf he acted as agent in the sales of several French art collections that now constitute the major attractions of The Hermitage in Leningrad.

MUSÉE DU LOUVRE, PARIS

terns and his young brother Augustin an engraver. Gabriel himself remained obscure, ignored or laughed at by his contemporaries. Even Augustin regarded him as a gifted failure. "Rather than studying," he writes, "he followed his inclination." His inclination was "to spend his entire life drawing everything he found on his way." Eccentric, Bohemian, solitary, fiercely intent on preserving his privacy—like Watteau— he sketched in pen, pencil or watercolor the thousand passing events, fashions and scenes of Parisian life. The 18th Century had discovered time, invented the moment; here at last was the swift, light, elegant, newsy hand needed to capture it.

Saint-Aubin is the Watteau of journalism. The fugitive, the evanescent aspects of life are caught and set aglow by his brush much as moths rush into a flame and are seared. His overwhelming passion for drawing drove him gradually to give up painting and etching, to neglect his health and his appearance; when he died his rooms were such a filthy clutter that the notary public refused to make an inventory of them. Yet in those rooms lay the countless fragile leaves and pads which were to perpetuate the memory of 18th Century life. In fact, many paintings of the age have come down to us only because Saint-Aubin sketched them in the margins of auction and Salon catalogues.

Watteau, Chardin, Saint-Aubin were outsiders. There was one signal exception: Jean-Honoré Fragonard. Not only his palette was rosy, his life was as well. He was, in fact, born virtually in a bed of roses: at Grasse, which was then, and still is, one enormous flower bed—a center for the perfume industry. There were perfumers in Fragonard's family; his father, however, was a glovemaker. Unfortunately, the elder Fragonard was also a gullible speculator: he sank his savings into one of those financial mirages which Paris excelled in conjuring up. Having come to the capital, around 1740, to collect the remainders of his investments, he was forced to remain as an employee in a haberdashery. Young Jean-Honoré was placed as a clerk in a lawyer's office. But not for long; the lawyer himself suggested that he become a painter—less an indication of his artistic flair, perhaps, than of his eagerness to get rid of a boy who filled every empty margin with scribbles. For Fragonard must already have fallen prey to that veritable rage to draw and to paint which possessed him well into old age, impelling him to work with anything that fell under his hand: pencil, pen, knife, brush, brush handle. "I would paint with my posterior," he once said.

His parents took him to Boucher, who passed him on to Chardin. After a few months, the latter wisely sent him back to Boucher, who now accepted him as a student—the most gifted, indeed, to be trained in his studio. What Watteau had been to Boucher, Boucher now was to Fragonard. Together, the three form that great triptych of love which is the 18th Century's most typical creation.

Boucher advised his disciple to compete for the Prix de Rome. Although only 20 years old, he won it on his first try in 1752; and four years later he departed for Italy. His old master did not see him leave without apprehension. He had guessed that fire and impatience were the essence of Fragonard's personality; how would they bear up under the

Jean-Jacques Rousseau's philosophy was clearly at odds with that of many of his contemporaries. Theirs was materialistic and based on reason while his was deistic and founded on sentiment. Rousseau believed that man was virtuous at heart and was corrupted only by the social order—by property, inequality and despotism.

heavy yoke of academic training, based—now as in Le Brun's time—on the slavish copying of antiquity, the masters of the High Renaissance, and the Bolognese School? "If you take Michelangelo and Raphael seriously, you are a lost fellow," Boucher had warned Fragonard.

His fear was justified. After a few months of the schoolish diet at the French Academy in Rome, Fragonard seemed to have lost his fire and, with it, all his ability. There is no telling what might have happened had he not struck up a warm friendship with another young Frenchman at the Academy, Hubert Robert. The latter's interest in antiquity was anything but slavish; he bet his friend six pads of drawing paper that he would climb the Colosseum from the outside, did so one night, and planted a cross on the top as a memorial of his feat. Fragonard followed his ebullient friend into the streets of Rome and the surrounding countryside. The sight of popular life jolted him from his studious, sterile routine. He became more attentive to Italian artists whose *brio* was closer to his own nature: Pietro da Cortona, Solimena, and above all Tiepolo. More than any painters, however, it was nature that set him right; it is in the sketches of the bowers and fountains of the Villa d'Este, at Tivoli, which he visited at length with Robert and their common patron and friend, the Abbé de Saint-Non, one of those devoted amateurs of art that the century produced again and again, that we meet for the first time the real Fragonard.

In 1761, after five years of absence, he returned to Paris. It was high time to make himself known. The first step was to become a member of the Academy. Fragonard executed a work so stilted and uninspired that it won him unanimous admission: *The High Priest Coresus Sacrificing Himself to Save Callirrhoe.* When the picture was exhibited at the Salon, it satisfied the experts but proved as tedious to the public as it had been to the painter.

Fragonard did not hesitate; he turned his back on the experts, who were soon discouraged by the "flimsiness" of his production. His inclinations and his interest conveniently coincided; he wanted to paint frivolous subjects, which was also what the rich were prepared to buy. By 1764, Pompadour had died; the court had been bitten by the Greek bug. But the world of parvenus and demimondaines remained attached to the themes and style that had been established by Boucher. Fragonard became their favorite supplier. Whenever a tax collector wished to offer a rakish scene to the ballerina of his desire—a naked lass teasing her lapdog, a damsel feebly defending her virtue—he thought of Fragonard.

Those who did not were soon set straight, as the following story shows. A rich personage had called in the painter Doyen. Pointing to a young woman with whom he clearly was on terms of intimacy, he explained to the artist that he would like him to depict her soaring high on a swing pushed by a bishop, while he himself would be reclining in the grass, savoring the spicy spectacle of flying skirts. Doyen was taken aback, not so much by the nature of the request as by the fact that it should be addressed to him, a painter of religious scenes. He referred the man to Fragonard. The result was the giddiest swing of a century that, taking Watteau's cue, had produced dozens *(pages 182-183)*.

Catering to fashion entailed the obligation to follow that fickle lady in her successive whims. But what others would have regarded as a painful imposition was a pleasure for Fragonard. His inconstancy and impatience delighted in change. When everybody longed for the simple country life he turned gleefully from boudoir to barn. He swung himself from "petty virtue"—the age's euphemism for vice—to authentic virtue by dint of his incomparable virtuosity. He painted scenes of faithful wedlock and happy family life as easily as he depicted the embraces of lovers. Were virtue and innocence the fashion? His brush gave birth to hordes of endearing infants at play or at school. For these he found convenient models at home; he had married a girl from Grasse who bore him two children, Rosalie and Evariste.

By all the rules Fragonard should have been a victim of his age. Yet he was one of its greatest masters. His work, conceived by its creator as a strictly timely art, now appears timeless. How could this happen?

The answer lies in Fragonard's very special artistic qualities. Let us turn again to *The Swing*. It tells a story of lightness, frivolity and superficiality, and as such it is the very quintessence of the century. But it is more than just that. The motion of the swing, its delicious but momentary pause at the apex of its course are not merely the subject of Fragonard's work; they are its very substance and style. Lightness and mobility, the foibles of the age, have become the artist's forte. His hand is faster and lighter than the women it sketches.

Indeed, it is probably the swiftest hand in the history of painting, swifter even than that of the painters whom he most admired: Rembrandt, Hals, Rubens, Tiepolo. The acceleration of time, as we have seen, had made the 18th Century discover time. Watteau foresaw it, Fragonard lived it. The dizzying velocity of his hand enables him to ride the crest of time's wave. His pencil zigzags about the piece of paper with the speed of lightning, picking a shepherd, a statue, a branch, a camel or a dog out of the void, yet never stopping or lingering on any one object, never grounding itself. The brush wanders impetuously about the surface of the canvas, seeming to leave behind it a wake of highly inflammable powder; the painter sets fire to it (*All in a Blaze* is in fact the title of one of his oils) and instantly the picture goes up in flames.

Mere virtuosity? Perhaps. But in the process something unprecedented happens, something of which Boucher has only given us a premonitory glimpse. Until now, painting, the artist's craft, has been at the service of the subject to be represented. Suddenly this relationship is reversed. Forms and strokes are no longer fettered by a world that must be depicted. That world lies, weighty and motionless, behind the surface of the canvas as behind a windowpane. Fragonard does not seek to strike through the surface of the pane, he accepts superficiality, makes use of it. At times he skates on it, at others he douses it, as a charwoman floods the kitchen floor, with fluid pigment. Take Fragonard's fabulous foliages; their leaves seem to multiply before our very eyes, to bubble over with elation, they become buoyant and volatile like clouds, dilate like the balloons that the brothers Montgolfier were sending skyward in those same years. Thanks to Fragonard, painting has at last overcome gravity.

Much art of the 18th Century is known only because of the artist Gabriel de Saint-Aubin's hobby. He attended sales and exhibitions and drew tiny postage-stamp-sized reproductions of the paintings in the margins of the catalogues, as this page shows. Saint-Aubin is better known for these sketches than for his own paintings, which were, nevertheless, very accomplished.

The less the world weighs, the easier it is to shrug it off. Unquestionably Fragonard's place in time helped him to free himself. Watteau was preserved because he came too early; Fragonard was saved because he came too late—an outsider after all. The party was turning into a memory. Watteau imagined a world that was soon to become real; when Fragonard appeared, that world was nearly reduced to a phantasm.

So flimsy was Fragonard's subject matter that it allowed him to travel light. Even in his portraits, his subjective fancy prevailed over objective fidelity to the model. Despite the fact that the Abbé de Saint-Non and his brother, M. de La Bretèche, sat for two of his most superb pictures *(page 176-177)*—each was "executed in an hour's time" as it swaggeringly says on their backs—they are rightly called *"portraits de fantaisie."* But what this fantasy really means is that manner has established its supremacy over matter, that the hand could henceforth move according to its own whims—in short, that painting had discovered freedom. These canvases are faithful portraits after all: portraits of painting itself, on the day of its emancipation, flushed and almost breathless with the excitement of its self-discovery, leaping about joyously like a colt let loose for the first time. It was more than a reversal, it was a revolution. To a certain extent all modern art (not just Goya, Manet or Renoir) insofar as it exalts the act of painting at the expense—and finally to the exclusion—of the facts to be depicted, owes its existence to Fragonard.

The end of the French monarchy marked the triumph of the frozen neoclassicism of Jacques-Louis David and his school and Fragonard lost the favor of the public. The discomforts of poverty thus came together with those of old age. But Fragonard's setbacks did not make him lose his good humor. When the revolutionary government cut down by two thirds the pension he had been receiving, he danced a jig. "Are you mad?" exclaimed his wife, whom he called "The Cashier." "No, I am happy," he replied. "They could have cut off our pension entirely!"

Fragonard returned to Grasse, for about a year, in 1790 during the Reign of Terror. The trip may have been precautionary; Fragonard had been associated with the hated Du Barry, Louis XV's last mistress, and the libertine financiers and ballerinas who were the very symbol of the ruinous vices of the *ancien régime.* By 1792, he was back in Paris. He had practically ceased to work. But David, remembering that he had once been under Fragonard's influence, now extended his all-powerful protection to him. Fragonard was named member and soon president of the Museum Commission; he no longer painted, but he was able to protect and to save the paintings of the past. It was enough to keep him happy. Marguerite Gérard, his sister-in-law, called him "a child whom a trifle saddens and a trifle appeases, a real, capricious baby." He died in 1806, felled by a stroke while eating ice cream.

Struck down while eating ice cream! That is how the glittering society first portrayed by Watteau might be said to have ended. There had been plenty of omens. Again and again, through the century, the dark cry of "Bread! We want bread!" had been raised outside the fence-protected enchanted park. Twenty years before the Revolution, Voltaire had written to a friend: "We shall lapse into the excessive, the colossal. . . ." The gayest people is also the most barbarous, he had warned scores of times; the monkeys will turn into tigers. Nor was such foresight a monopoly of philosophers. One Sunday in 1763, the priest of Saint-Eustache proclaimed in his sermon: "Sooner or later, the revolution will break out."

The signs of doom were unmistakable, but could those whom it threatened be expected to read them? Not even the revolutionaries did. As Talleyrand, one of the protagonists of this historical drama, said afterward: "One would not go so far if one knew where one was going." Butterflies make bad prophets and worse reformers. To the very last moment they practiced what they knew: unthinking elegance and grace.

And when the flood came, the only vessel on which they could take flight was Watteau's Cytherean ship. It was too frail an ark to save them and their culture. Voltaire's valedictory now took on its full significance: "Goodbye beautiful verse, goodbye feelings of the heart, goodbye all." Only a handful of survivors could remember, testify, and mourn. "Where will such a society ever be found again?" sighed the moribund Prince de Ligne in faraway Vienna. "France has ceased laughing," bitterly noted the exiled polemicist Rivarol, in Hamburg. "Woman ruled France, the Revolution dethroned her," wrote Mme. Vigée-Lebrun, the court portraitist, who traveled about Europe, carrying with her a portrait of Marie-Antoinette, a black ribbon tied to it. But the *mot de la fin* must be left to the most intelligent turncoat in history, Talleyrand: "He who has not lived before the Revolution does not know the sweetness of living."

The generations who rose later—the people of the Revolution and the Napoleonic Empire—had not, of course, lived then: from them, the 18th Century could only expect misunderstanding, contempt or indifference. Fragonard's own son, who was then studying with David, burned his father's magnificent collection of contemporary prints. "I am offering a holocaust to good taste," he explained.

Hubert Robert's taste for the picturesque exactly fitted the mid-18th Century's penchant for the classical past. His specialties were monuments and ruins. This drawing shows a triumphal arch of the Roman Emperor Hadrian. Robert was also fond of depicting parks; he became so well known for this that in 1788 he was asked to design some royal gardens for the King.

171

Love's
Last Fling

The most poetic painter in the peak years of the sensual and voluptuous 18th Century was Jean-Honoré Fragonard, born, appropriately, in the fragrant perfume-making town of Grasse. It is mainly through his eyes that the modern world sees the final flowering of that age of pleasure, which he painted in Rococo pictures of swirling line and shimmering color. Into these paintings—which sold quickly and for handsome sums —Fragonard poured the wit, grace, joy in life and boundless delight in women that filled his French soul.

Fragonard's success was built on works he often painted to order, suiting the prevailing taste. When the fancy was for pastoral scenes, Fragonard filled his landscapes with gamboling sheep and coy shepherdesses. When portraits were in demand, he was able to turn them out almost as swiftly as if—in the words of one expert—"the wind itself had painted them." For the naughty taste he painted delicate and delicious boudoir pictures like the one at right, and for the virtuous he fashioned joyful scenes of glowing motherhood. But with all his facile flexibility, Fragonard never relaxed his artistic demands upon himself. He remained throughout his career a masterful technician. Even when he neglected to model a hand or limb fully, he always managed to capture the pulsing life of his subject. For an age of momentary pleasures and quick delights, Fragonard was a perfect spokesman.

Resisting, but not too strongly,
a maiden pulls halfheartedly
away from a furtive kiss
in one of the artist's many
evocations of romantic love.

Fragonard: *The Stolen Kiss*, late 1780s

Fragonard: *The Useless Resistance,* early 1770s

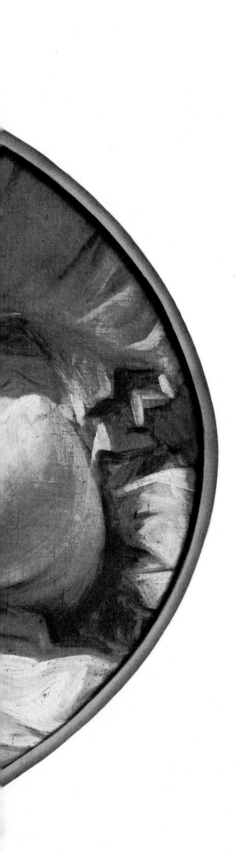

Fragonard: *First Lesson in Horsemanship*, c. 1782

Fragonard studied art under two great masters of his day —Chardin and Boucher. The first, Chardin, tried to teach the young man his own careful methods: "You search, you scumble, you glaze," he instructed. But Fragonard's temperament was not suited to such a methodical approach. He preferred the exciting lessons of Boucher, who taught pragmatically, brush in hand, exhorting his pupils to paint as quickly as himself, to be bold in line and brave in color. The master had special instructions for those who would paint the female nude: "We must not think of a woman's body as a covering for bones. It should not be fat though it certainly should be rounded; it should be firm and slender without thereby appearing to be thin." And although Boucher reserved his best model for himself, at least one of his students learned about females splendidly, as the picture at left shows. In time, Fragonard began to exploit this skill in works like *Kiss on the Neck* and *The Stolen Shift*. These provocative scenes would have been shameless except, as the historian brothers Goncourt noted, for their "unique charm of partial revelation. . . . His decency," they observed, "consists in the lightness of his touch. His colors are not the pigments of a painter but the suggestions of a poet."

For all his preoccupations with erotic love, Fragonard never neglected the domestic virtues. In the drawing above, one of many depictions of the education of children, the same poetry that infuses his boudoir dramas keeps the scene from becoming mawkish. The special charm of this delicate sketch is that it shows the artist himself with his wife and young son.

Fragonard: *Portrait of the Abbé de Saint-Non*, 1769

Supremely confident of his own skills, Fragonard delighted in astounding fellow artists and friends with his virtuoso handling of a brush. He painted their portraits "at one fell swoop for one louis," but the coin was the smallest part of his satisfaction.

He called these small pictures—most measure roughly two and a half by two feet—"portraits of fantasy." Sitters for them had the fun of dressing up in theatrical costumes and the added treat of watching Fragonard at work. One of them, shown at left above, was Jean-Claude Richard de Saint-Non, abbot of a monastery, a counselor to Parliament and a close friend of the artist's, as well as an important patron. Sitting for the master in the dashing clothes of a cavalier must have been a special pleasure for Saint-Non since he was himself a talented amateur artist—his pastels are so good that they are often mistaken for Fragonard's. M. de La Bretèche, his brother *(lower left)*, is pictured not as the debonair aristocrat he was but as a musician strumming his guitar. The brothers' portraits are believed to have been designed to hang together, possibly above a doorway since the subjects are painted from slightly below eye level.

An example of the remarkable artistic shorthand Fragonard developed is shown in the detail at right from the portrait of Saint-Non. With swirls of creamy white he creates the feathery plume in the corner; a single slash of yellow ochre—replacing careful modeling—highlights the back and knuckles of the right hand, bending it into shadow. In addition to this evidence of his deftness, inscriptions on the backs of both works confirm that each was "painted by Fragonard in one hour's time." He was even stenographic in adding his signature; one of his few dated works, the La Bretèche portrait is signed "Frago, 1769."

Fragonard: *Portrait of M. de La Bretèche*, 1769

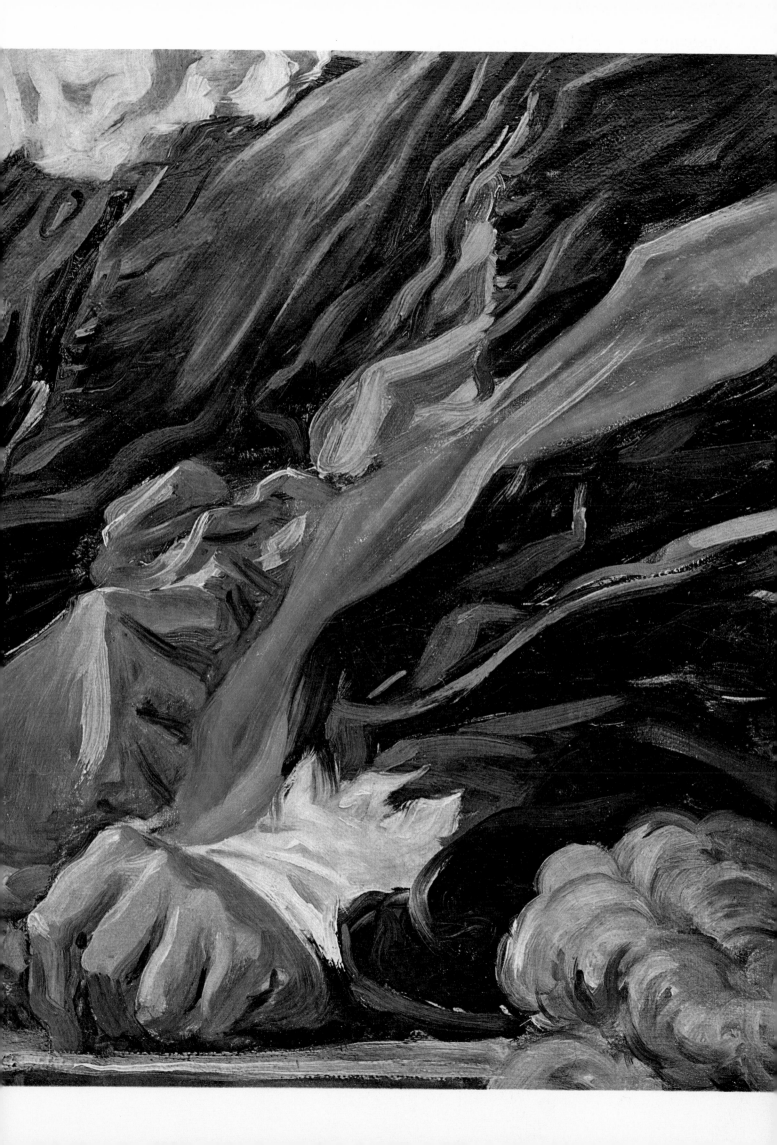

Such was Fragonard's confidence that he could paint in many modes. Alert to the work of his contemporaries and knowledgeable about his predecessors, Fragonard, like Chardin, painted scenes of family life; like Hubert Robert he did landscapes, and he used pastoral and love themes like those painted by his chief inspirer, Boucher. At the beginning of his career he had painted a convincingly religious *Adoration of the Shepherds,* and later he did a number of *fêtes galantes* in the tradition of the greatest master of the era, Watteau.

In no instance did Fragonard imitate the work of others; he simply set out to tackle their subject matter in his personal manner. Compared with Watteau's quiet, moody *fêtes galantes,* for example, Fragonard's *Fête at Rambouillet (right)* is an extravaganza of fantasy. Gay aristocrats frolic in elaborately decorated boats before a château whose walls are somehow made of trees. Dramatic backlighting and the jagged lines of gnarled branches add an unsettling drama to the scene. There is no mistaking this work for a Watteau; it is Fragonard's own curiously dissonant, typically fantastic, treatment of the pleasures of his gay but troubled world—a world which was to be torn by revolution in a few years.

Fragonard: *Fête at Rambouillet*, c. 1780

Fragonard: *The Meeting*, 1771-1773.

Louis XV's last mistress, Madame Du Barry, an unlucky charmer destined to die upon the guillotine, bought Fragonard's paintings but proved a difficult customer. To decorate the walls of one of her pleasure domes, Du Barry chose as a theme Loves of the Shepherds, and commissioned Fragonard to paint four panels—*The Pursuit, The Meeting, Love Letters* and *The Lover Crowned*—two of which are shown here. While Fragonard was at work on the series, Du Barry constantly interrupted him, suggesting changes and rearrangements

Fragonard: *The Lover Crowned*, 1771-1773.

until finally, wearily, he finished them. Inexplicably, the paintings were then rejected and Fragonard disdainfully refused the 18,000 livres he had been promised. Perhaps the Countess had not liked them, or they had not been erotic enough to suit the jaded King, or they had not fitted the architect's plans. Fragonard was evidently greatly attached to the paintings; he kept them in his studio for almost 20 years, and when he left Paris during the Terror he took them along to decorate the drawing room of a cousin's house in his old home town, Grasse.

181

Fragonard: *The Swing*, 1766

The age of the Rococo finally died with the Revolution; tastes changed, many wealthy collectors died, and France's economy was in a turmoil. An old tradition of classicism rose to dominance again under the guidance of Jacques-Louis David, Fragonard's friend, whose vote helped send the King to the chopping block and whose pictures of Roman patriotism stirred the populace. Fragonard's elegant poetry was no longer needed; his spirit was that of a different time. Although he was given a position on a committee to establish a national collection of art treasures, changes in government led to his resignation and after a few years of dwindling finances, he died. At his death he was politely "esteemed," and faintly praised for his "frivolous, erotic" subjects.

Not words but a picture best summarizes both Fragonard's art and his time. His painting *The Swing,* shown here, was made to order for a lovesick baron and expresses, for better or worse, the morality and the spirit of the age: pushed by a bishop, a mademoiselle kicks off her slipper while her lover swoons from exquisite pleasure. Under Fragonard's brush the delicious moment has become an eternal one.

Chronology: Artists of the 17th and 18th Centuries

1550 — 1650 — 1750 — 1850   1550 — 1650 — 1750 — 1850

FRANCE

LE NAIN FRÈRES fl. 1588-1677

GEORGES DE LA TOUR 1593-1652

NICOLAS POUSSIN c. 1594-1665

FRANÇOIS MANSART 1598-1666

CLAUDE LORRAIN 1600-1682

PHILIPPE DE CHAMPAIGNE 1602-1674

LOUIS LE VAU 1612(?)-1670

PIERRE MIGNARD 1612-1695

ANDRÉ LE NÔTRE 1613-1700

CLAUDE PERRAULT 1613-1688

CHARLES LE BRUN 1619-1690

PIERRE PUGET 1620-1694

FRANÇOIS GIRARDON 1628-1715

CHARLES DE LA FOSSE 1636-1716

JEAN BERAIN 1637-1711

ANTOINE COYZEVOX 1640-1720

JULES HARDOUIN MANSART 1646-1708

JEAN-BAPTISTE SANTERRE 1651-1717

NICOLAS DE LARGILLIÈRE 1656-1746

CLAUDE AUDRAN III 1658-1734

HYACINTHE RIGAUD 1659-1743

ANTOINE COYPEL 1661-1722

FRANÇOIS DESPORTES 1661-1743

JACQUES GABRIEL V 1667-1742

CLAUDE GILLOT 1673-1722

ANTOINE WATTEAU 1684-1721

JEAN MARC NATTIER 1685-1766

JEAN-BAPTISTE OUDRY 1686-1755

FRANÇOIS LE MOINE 1688-1737

NOËL-NICOLAS COYPEL 1690-1734

NICOLAS LANCRET 1690-1745

JEAN-BAPTISTE PATER 1695-1736

JACQUES-ANGE GABRIEL 1698-1782

JEAN-BAPTISTE SIMÉON CHARDIN 1699-1779

JEAN ÉTIENNE LIOTARD (SWISS) 1702-1789

FRANÇOIS BOUCHER 1703-1770

MAURICE QUENTIN DE LATOUR 1704-1788

CARLE VAN LOO 1705-1765

JOSEPH VERNET 1714-1789

JEAN-BAPTISTE PERRONNEAU 1715-1783

ÉTIENNE-MAURICE FALCONET 1716-1791

PIERRE-ANTOINE BAUDOUIN 1723-1769

GABRIEL DE SAINT-AUBIN 1724-1780

JEAN-BAPTISTE GREUZE 1725-1805

JEAN-HONORÉ FRAGONARD 1732-1806

HUBERT ROBERT 1733-1808

CLODION 1738-1814

JEAN ANTOINE HOUDON 1741-1828

JACQUES-LOUIS DAVID 1748-1825

ÉLISABETH VIGÉE-LEBRUN 1755-1842

HOLLAND

FRANS HALS 1580-1666

HENDRICK TERBRUGGHEN 1588-1629

JAN VAN GOYEN 1596-1656

ADRIAEN BROUWER 1605/06-1638

REMBRANDT HARMENSZ. VAN RIJN 1606-1669

ADRIAEN VAN OSTADE 1610-1684

GERARD TERBORCH 1617-1681

JAN STEEN 1626-1679

PIETER DE HOOGH 1629-1683

JACOB VAN RUISDAEL c. 1630-1681

JAN VERMEER 1632-1675

MEINDERT HOBBEMA 1638-1709

SPAIN

JUSEPE RIBERA 1588-1652

FRANCISCO DE ZURBURÁN 1598-1664

DIEGO VELÁSQUEZ 1599-1660

BARTOLOMÉ-ESTEBAN MURILLO 1617-1682

FRANCISCO GOYA 1746-1828

FLANDERS

PETER PAUL RUBENS 1577-1640

JACOB JORDAENS 1593-1678

ANTHONY VAN DYCK 1599-1641

DAVID TENIERS THE YOUNGER 1610-1690

ITALY

MICHELANGELO MERISI DA CARAVAGGIO 1560/65-1609

ANNIBALE CARRACCI 1560-1609

GUIDO RENI 1575-1642

GUERCINO 1591-1666

PIETRO DA CORTONA 1596-1669

GIOVANNI LORENZO BERNINI 1598-1680

FRANCESCO BORROMINI 1599-1667

ALESSANDRO MAGNASCO c. 1677-1749

GIAMBATTISTA PIAZZETTA 1682-1754

GIOVANNI BATTISTA TIEPOLO 1696-1770

GIOVANNI ANTONIO CANALETTO 1697-1768

FRANCESCO GUARDI 1712-1793

GIOVANNI BATTISTA PIRANESI 1720-1778

ENGLAND

GODFREY KNELLER 1646-1723

RICHARD WILSON 1714-1782

JOSHUA REYNOLDS 1723-1792

THOMAS GAINSBOROUGH 1727-1788

GEORGE ROMNEY 1734-1802

UNITED STATES

JOHN SINGLETON COPLEY 1737-1815

BENJAMIN WEST 1738-1820

CHARLES WILLSON PEALE 1741-1827

GILBERT STUART 1755-1828

1550 — 1650 — 1750 — 1850   1550 — 1650 — 1750 — 1850

Watteau's predecessors and contemporaries are grouped chronologically according to country. The bands correspond to the life-spans of the artists.

Bibliography *Available in paperback

WATTEAU—HIS LIFE AND WORK

Adhémar, Hélène and René Huyghe, *Watteau*. Tisné, Paris, 1950. The important monograph on Watteau; in French.

Dacier, Emile and Albert Vuaflart, *Jean de Jullienne et les graveurs de Watteau au XVIIIe siècle*, 4 vols. Société pour l'étude de la gravure française, Paris, 1921-29. Annotated edition of engravings made after Watteau's work and published by his friend and patron.

Mathey, J., *Antoine Watteau: Peintures Réapparues*. F. de Nobele, Paris, 1959. An authoritative discussion of Watteau's career with evidence for the attribution of some works.

Parker, K. T. and J. Mathey, *Antoine Watteau: Catalogue complet de son oeuvre dessiné*, 2 vols. Société de reproduction de dessins anciens et modernes, Paris, 1957. A complete catalogue with reproductions of Watteau's drawings.

Rosenberg, Jakob, *Great Draughtsmen from Pisanello to Picasso* (pages 85-100). Harvard University Press, Cambridge, 1959. Unique critical insights into Watteau's work, especially his draftsmanship.

OTHER ARTISTS OF THE TIME

Besnard, Albert, *La Tour: la vie et l'oeuvre de l'artiste* (catalogue critique par Georges Wildenstein). Beaux-Arts, Paris, 1928. A biography of the artist with an illustrated catalogue by Georges Wildenstein; in French.

Goncourt, Edmond and Jules de, *French XVIII Century Painters*. Phaidon, London, 1948. Six illuminating essays by two 19th Century men of letters.

Ingersoll-Smouse, Florence, *Pater*. Beaux-Arts, Paris, 1928. The basic study of Pater and his work.

Mauclair, Camille, *Greuze et son temps*. Alban Michel, Paris, 1926. A dated but able study in French.

Michel, André, *François Boucher*. Librairie de l'art, Paris, 1929. One of the few biographies of this painter; in French.

Rosenberg, Pierre, *Chardin*. Translated from the French by Helga Harrison. Skira, Geneva, 1963.

Wildenstein, Georges, *Chardin*. Manesse, Zurich, 1963. A fine interpretation with a well-illustrated catalogue; in French.

Lancret. Beaux-Arts, Paris, 1924.

The Paintings of Fragonard. Translated from the French by C. W. Chilton and Mrs. A. L. Kitson. Phaidon, London, 1960. A scholarly monograph, illustrated and with a complete catalogue.

SOCIAL AND HISTORICAL BACKGROUND

*Boulenger, Jacques, *The Seventeenth Century in France*. Translated from the French. G. P. Putnam's Sons, New York, 1963. A readable history.

Carsten, F. D., ed., *The New Cambridge Modern History: The Ascendancy of France 1648-88*, vol. V. Cambridge University Press, Cambridge, 1961. An indispensable reference book for the art, literature and history of the times.

*Cobban, Alfred, *A History of Modern France* (vol. 1: 1715-1799). Penguin, Baltimore, 1963. Includes a particularly good essay on the *ancien régime*.

Goncourt, Edmond and Jules de, *The Woman of the 18th Century*. Translated from the French by Jacques Le Clercq and Ralph Roeder. Minton Balch, New York, 1927. Amusing and keen observations on the society of the time.

Gooch, G. P., *Louis XV: The Monarchy in Decline*. Longman, Green, London, 1956. A scholarly and clear account of his reign.

Guérard, Albert, *The Life and Death of an Ideal: France in the Classical Age*. Georges Braziller, New York, 1956. A reliable history of the 16th to the 18th Centuries.

*Hazard, Paul, *The European Mind 1680-1715*. Meridian, Cleveland, 1963. A classic study of the intellectual life of the period.

Lacroix, Paul, *France in the Eighteenth Century: Its Institutions, Customs and Costumes*. Frederick Ungar, New York, republished 1963. First published in 1876.

*Lewis, W. H., *The Splendid Century: Life in the France of Louis XIV*. Doubleday, New York, 1957. A readable and informative history.

The Sunset of the Splendid Century. Doubleday, New York, 1963.

Lindsay, J. O., ed., *The New Cambridge Modern History: The Old Regime 1713-63*. Cambridge University Press, Cambridge, 1957. A reliable and complete history of Louis XIV, the Regency, and Louis XV.

Montesquieu, Charles de, *Persian Letters*. Translated by G. R. Healy. Bobbs-Merrill, Indianapolis, 1964. Observations of Paris and the Parisians of the 18th Century through the eyes of two fictitious Persian visitors.

Nicoll, Allardyce, *Masks, Mimes and Miracles*. Cooper Square, New York, 1963. A history of the popular theater.

The World of Harlequin. Cambridge University Press, Cambridge, 1963. A lively, readable study of the *commedia dell'arte*.

Nolhac, Pierre de, *Versailles and the Trianons*. Illustrated by René Binet. Heinemann, London, 1906. A charmingly illustrated volume written by a curator of Versailles.

Saint-Simon, *Mémoires*, 4 vols. Gallimard, Paris, 1950. A voluminous and detailed record of court life written by a nobleman in the mid-18th Century.

Schönberger, Arno and Halldor Soehner, with the collaboration of Theodor Müller, *The Rococo Age: Art and Civilization of the 18th Century*. Translated from the German by Daphne Woodward. Thames and Hudson, London, 1960. A general, informative survey, well-illustrated.

Voltaire, *Age of Louis XIV*. Translated by Martyn P. Pollack. Everyman's Library Edition. Dutton, New York.

Lettres choisies. Garnier, Paris, 1963. Selected letters.

HISTORY OF ART

Adhémar, Jean, *Graphic Art of the 18th Century*. Translated from the French by M. I. Martin. McGraw-Hill, New York, 1964. An important history of the evolution of the print.

Blunt, Anthony, *Art and Architecture in France 1500-1700*. Penguin, Baltimore, 1954. Interesting and concise.

Fosca, François, *The Eighteenth Century: Watteau to Tiepolo*. Translated by Stuart Gilbert. Skira, New York, 1952. A general survey.

French Cabinet-Makers of the XVIIIth Century. Preface by Pierre Verlet. Hachette, Paris, 1965. Well-illustrated and important to an understanding of the social history of the times.

Honour, Hugh, *Chinoiserie*. John Murray, London, 1961. An interesting discussion of a major 18th Century vogue.

*Kimball, Fiske, *The Creation of the Rococo*. Norton, New York, 1964. A scholarly work on the development of this artistic style.

Kitson, Michael, *The Age of the Baroque*. McGraw-Hill, New York, 1966. A pictorial compilation.

Les porcelainiers du XVIIIe siècle français. Préface de Serge Gauthier. Hachette, Paris, 1964. A beautifully illustrated account of porcelain production in 18th Century France.

*Levey, Michael, *Rococo to Revolution*. Praeger, New York, 1966. Illuminating essays on the styles of European art in the 18th Century.

Marcel, Pierre, *La Peinture Française au début du XVIIIe siècle 1690-1721*. Quantin, Paris, c. 1910. An excellent and informative study of the period. Out of print.

Thuillier, Jacques and Albert Châtelet, *French Painting: From Le Nain to Fragonard*. Translated from the French by James Emmons. Skira, Geneva, 1964. A recent authoritative survey, well-illustrated.

Wilenski, R. H., *French Painting*. Charles T. Branford, Boston, 1949. Though dated, still useful.

Acknowledgments

For their help in the production of this book the editors wish to acknowledge the following people: Madame Hélène Adhémar, Conservateur des Musées du Jeu de Paume et de L'Orangerie, Paris; the authorities of the Wallace Collection, London; Catherine Belenger, Service des Relations Extérieures du Musée du Louvre; Per Bjurström, Deputy Keeper, National Museum of Fine Arts, Stockholm; Madame Yane Bonéfant, Attachée au Cabinet des Estampes de la Bibliothèque Nationale, Paris; Helmut Börsch-Supan, Verwaltung der Staatlichen Schlösser und Gärten, Berlin-Charlottenburg; Marcel Brandin, Chef de Cabinet, Ministère des Affaires Culturelles, Paris; Arlette Calvé, Assistante au Cabinet des Dessins du Musée du Louvre; Jean de Cayeux, Paris; Marie-Louise Cornillot, Conservateur, Musée de Besançon; the Curators of Prints and Drawings, The Morgan Library, New York; Department of Prints, The Metropolitan Museum of Art, New York; David Finch, French Institute, New York; The Frick Art Reference Library, New York; The Frick Collection, New York; Pontus Grate, Curator, National Museum of Fine Arts, Stockholm; Madame Guynet-Pechadre, Conservateur, Service Photographique, Musée du Louvre; Wilhelm Köhler, Gemaeldegalerie, Staatliche Museen zu Berlin; Kupferstichkabinet, Staatliche Museen zu Berlin; Jacqueline Le Clerc, Service des Relations Extérieures du Musée du Louvre; Pierre Lemoine, Conservateur, Château de Versailles; Henner Menz, Gemaeldegalerie Alter Meister, Dresden; Marc Saltet, Architecte en Chef, Conservateur du Domaine National de Versailles; Maurice Sérullaz and Roseline Bacou, Conservateurs du Cabinet des Dessins du Musée du Louvre; Max Seydewitz, Staatliche Kunstsammlungen, Dresden; Stephan Waetzoldt, Director, Staatliche Museen zu Berlin.

Picture Credits

Index

Numerals in italics indicate a picture. Unless otherwise identified, all listed art works are by Watteau. Titles of certain of Watteau's paintings are given in English and French. Dimensions are given in inches; height precedes width.

189

*The typeface employed in this book is called Janson, after Anton Janson, the Dutch
typefounder who popularized it in Leipzig in the late 17th Century. The face was first
cut, however, by Nicholas Kis, a Hungarian working in Amsterdam in the 1680s.*

✕

PRODUCTION STAFF FOR TIME INCORPORATED
*John L. Hallenbeck (Vice President and Director of Production),
Robert E. Foy, Caroline Ferri and Robert E. Fraser
Text photocomposed under the direction of Albert J. Dunn and Arthur J. Dunn*